From the Joy of Mount Shasta

Street·Wise Ascension

Ascending Daily Life on Main Street

Yoj Chase

Street·Wise Ascension

ISBN 978-0-9796723-5-4

© Copyright 2010 by Yoj Chase

English Publication - November 2010

Mount Shasta Light Publishing
PO Box 1509
Mount Shasta CA 96067-1509 – USA

Phone: 530-926-4599
Fax: 530-926-4159

E-mail: aurelia@mslpublishing.com
Web Site: www.mslpublishing.com
Also: www.lemurianconnection.com

All rights reserved

Cover Art: Tracy Tuttle
www.tracytuttledesign.com
Photography: Victoria Lee and Aurelia Louise Jones
Cover Design: Aaron Rose
Page Layout and Formatting: Aaron Rose
Editing: Christine Burk
Proofreading: Christi Albouy

Printed in the USA

I'm so, so very grateful to be a part and aware of your "flow" now. Your poetry, your Wisdom just pours through me, feeds me. Thank you so much.
Lady Mary ~ USA

I appreciate your short blasts of light each day! They resonate truth with me.
Jessica ~ Center of it All

This message again was simply beautiful. Thank you for being kind enough to share it with us.
Ted ~ USA

I always enjoy your beautiful messages...they are so powerful!
Iwetta ~ Berlin, Germany

Thank you so much for your rich and powerful messages! They truly bring music to my ears and remembrance to my soul. I have been so tired of conspiracy theories and repeated nonsense stories... and your messages have re-awakened and energized that part of me that already knows the Truth of why I am here now.
Victoria ~ Ontario, Canada

Thank you again Dear Brother Yoj, for reminding us—and setting an ever clarifying and expansive "Bar" for us realizing what's up—NOW.
Soldann ~ USA

Dear Shirley,
Your great love seems
to be there for me
- after, and
I thank you mum,
yours truly Yoj

*As Captain of my World
and for all other life,
I intend to embody
the fountain and reservoir
of Mother/Father God's
Cosmic Love to the Earth...*

*I Am one with this Way;
and this Way is filled with Cosmic Virtue,
with which I desire to bless the World.*

Publisher's Note:

Mount Shasta Light Publishing acknowledges and honors Yoj Chase's unique syntax, style, and languaging. The reader is encouraged to move freely "outside the box" with regard to standardized grammar and punctuation. Any misunderstandings or misapplications are the reader's responsibility.

It was a great pleasure to be a part of the unfolding of this specialized work.

Acknowledgments

- To the great Presence, my first love. To Its first expression understood by me: Its Infinite Circle of Light, the ongoing infinite One divided. To have something to love, I am so very grateful.

- To all the Angels, Elementals, and the Gathering of Ascended Humanity, for everything they give.

- To Andrew Bremness, for demonstrating poised Oneness flowing.

- To Patti Cota-Robles, for demonstrating the use of, and total connection to, the Presence.

- To the entire staff of "Ascended and Free," whose generous flow of Constant Illumination has been a constant for me and is reverb-ed throughout this Ministry and book.

- To Victoria Lee, who out-breathed the final vocalization of the One request to publish these.

- To Andy Aguilera, Chuck and Jason Young, and Richard Coots, for providing me the space and place of winter recreation/fun, disguised as "a job," which takes place on the slopes of Mount Shasta, where much of this inspiration came to mind.

- To my mom Dorothy and my sister Debbie, who have been ceaseless in their assistance.

- To John Thompson, Lisa Hampton, and Julie Crilley, for your hands-on help, inspiration, and personal assistance during the darkest of my days. Thanks for everything...!

- To Ahnee, for the constant goading to write.

- To Aaron Rose, for joyful cover design, page layout, and formatting of this book.

- To Michelle Anderson, for the constant feedback and use of these messages.

- To Beth Montgomery and Eugene Tsui, for providing me a residence to do this.

- And to every other individual who knows they gave a hand and that I am out of room to mention. I demand all that you've given to me be returned to you in an avalanche of glory. Also... *my song of Gratitude forever.*

Introduction

The Ascension of life is something that happens to all Worlds, to all Systems, and to all substance. We here on Earth have been in the dark, for a spell, regarding this real-time practical shift we have been preparing for. The way other worlds and the rest of the solar system enjoy preparing for the Great Shift is by educating the young and by speaking of it on the News. It is an *event* that must be *acknowledged and prepared for.* This is my/our intent and service here: to bring to "Main Street" the Power of Perfect Memories, in short full-bodied "blasts of Light" to assist any who may wish to contemplate or to utilize knowledge unto their benefit. This tome is spherical, and so it allows for "cutting into" anywhere.

These pages began as a daily email to a short list of friends. The emails were then forwarded around the globe. Over the months, several folks and families demanded that they be published for the public. Well, obedience seemed in order. Thus far, there are more than 180 messages. Those chosen to be included here seem to be of higher significance for the next Now Moment on Earth. I have simply tuned in to the "Universal I Am" and asked Its Desire to share **what really matters,** as would come forth from me, As One Presence acting.

What this flow of Wisdom seems to me to be, in short, is: This is You. It is the One/Self speaking back to you, the one/self here. And It means business.

As you know so well, gentle reader:
Now is the time to act like never before.

Throughout these messages the "Universal One" refers to you and me as "Masters." Contemplate this (is my suggestion). Somewhere in here it says something to the effect that *"only Masters are embodied here at this time, be they Masters of conflict or karmic games or be they Masters of Love Qualities. Everyone here at this time is accredited."* For me, what surrounds that information is both staggering and comforting to my mind and feelings. Also, it has answered many questions and observations about myself and the world.

I, of all men, am so blessed. And you are very much a piece of that blessing. Breathing praise and thanks to the Infinite, for your Love and Freedom, I thank you.

Yoj Chase
Mount Shasta, California
10-10-10

Note: Regarding the numbered degrees above each contemplation, I've chosen to give place to the step by step wisdom within the directive eluded to in all the great spiritual texts, which is:

Humanity, as a majority,
requires a *180° turn,*
back to the rule of Love
and Its Wisdom of Harmony,
if we intend Peace to prevail.

Prelude

A Note from the Ascended Jesus – The Christ

"There is an unfortunate tendency among the awakening ones to restrict members of the great Light Realms to various titles and non-expansive levels of being. Relax the tendency to categorize Angels, Ascended Masters, and multidimensional Extraterrestrials. Holy personages do not consider themselves as separate. In every sense we are One, You are One with Masters of Light as well. One does not reach levels of Christ Consciousness enlightenment through separative behavior. Creator is One integrated field of intelligent Light." *

Humanity will get this, either traveling happily or kicking and screaming its way into the immediate future. One of our Initiations is the knowing of equality, not in individual evolution, but in absolute Identity. Who You and We all are is the I AM – God in action – a Child of the Almighty, forever. This Truth has somehow been under wraps, though now, the wrapping has been torn off. Many truths still need acceptance. These writings are one grouping of many available designed to reveal Who we are – and our True Power.

* Excerpted by permission from *Arcturian Songs of the Masters of Light, Arcturian Star Chronicles Volume Four,* Beyond Words Publishing, Inc., © 1999 by Patricia L. Pereira

It is my sole intent that
every sentence of this book
assist the gentle reader in being
the one and only one in control
of their Feeling side of Life,
and to Be prepared for
the bigger shift at hand.

0°
Affirmations of True Identity

I Am a Force of Love Moving upon this Planet.

I Am an upward rushing Force
of Vibration and Consciousness,
which is my Heart Flame,
the True Center of my Being.

This Flame becomes
my Electronic Aura spiraling about me,
and Cosmic Energies flow through this Aura.

I Am a vast multidimensional
Being of Great Light,
and I Am One with all Light,
the Great Universal Consciousness.

So, I now wish to work with this gathering
and direct our Power to where it is needed most.
I ask from within my Heart that all the Light
entering my body through the crown
flow directly through my body
out the bottoms of my feet –
right into the core of Love
in the Center of this sweet Earth,
that She may do with it
whatever She chooses.

I ask that this be sustained
throughout this day
in all I do in Harmony.

I Am Grateful.

1°
Together Again!!

Perhaps We (always as One)
could take this moment together
and use our Superpower…
and with Bright Vibrant Visualization,
see and feel this – as a Now Moment of Truth:

A group of us are in a forest next to a creek;
birds and dragonflies abound. Ahh, mmm.
Suddenly a Cosmic hush, and stillness
drapes our whole space, all around.
In the clearing, a multi-tier
Starship of Peace appears.
The tall, lovely crew of 13 steps out:
8 women and 5 men.
We all bow to their great Light.
They in turn bow
to our great Light and Love.
They join our campfire and accept tea.
We are all smiling.

One of the men says,
"Do you know who you really are…?"
A woman begins to describe
the importance of that Truth.
Another man says, "We must begin immediately
to assist the oceans and the atmosphere."
So, the woman explains and describes how…

As our group settles in
to this real-time actuality,
the profound and overwhelming
Peace and Joy of Universal-Being-ness
becomes our Power and sustenance.

The Play and its work
have begun this step
of restoring this sweet Earth
and Her systems (our daily life)
back into alignment.
The Peace is unstoppable.
Our Family is re-united.
Our Mission is clear.
The animals weep for Joy.
The birds' songs are understood.
The task at hand is enormous.
Love, Wisdom, and Power (and Its Purity)
are the only things We obey – Ours.

*Remember I Am here, I Am there,
and I Am everywhere Present – right now.*

I Am Mother/Father God acting.

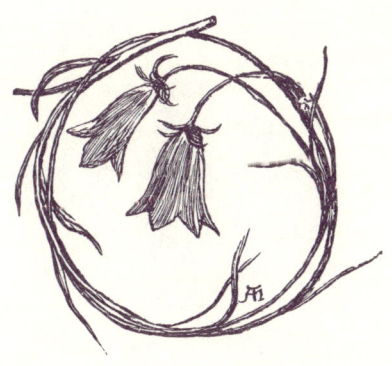

2°

It is good and it profits us
to return our attention
to the Fundamentals of Universal Being.
Our Hearts are the Throne Room
of God Consciousness,
literally a replica of the Great Central Sun.
We can have **anything** we want,
when we ask it from within the Heart.
Because, "Thou art God."

Who You are is the I AM
and your name is AUM (OM).
That is everybody's name, in reality.
You are here on this planet Now to manifest
an entirely "New Cosmic Reality":
Complete Freedom.
The race at large defends its fears
and some kill in defense of their fears.

Earth is a post-grad school.
This out-post is unlike any sphere
you have ever entered.
Everyone here, **on any mission,**
from anywhere, is a master.
Albeit, some are masters of karmic games,
masters of conflict, or control of others.
It matters not. Earth is exclusive
regarding its *all inclusiveness.*
Never have we seen this.

We bring this to the moment because
Prime Creator has taken a more direct hand
in Earth's Ascension process.
So we (as Source in action) must prepare
for more Patience than we think.

We, *The Masters of Love,*
are legend in the Universe.
We are the Deep, Deep Balance
and Passion, moving.

As your awakening (Light) increases,
so must your Gratitude.
Your Gratitude is so powerful,
we can scarcely put it into words.
Because we have already succeeded…
is one reason to practice greater patience.
Contemplate this, my beloved Self.
When the veils are removed,
our Joy will know no bounds.

3°

Beloved Co-Servers,
I bring you that which is most required
for your and for all Life's Freedom
from the destructive forces
working to achieve their own continuance.

We are the Systems Builders
and we also mean business.

Now, if every day you will just sit,
feel and call to your own great I Am,
then be still in your mind
and Visualize a Golden Sun
with the Amethyst Flame playing through
(the Gold and the Violet married as a Sun),
and demand with all of your heart's feeling
that this Vision, *which is real,*
be made a blessing to all Life here on Earth.
And declare that *all* the Host of Heaven
amplify this Presence to the maximum.
We will do it beyond your greatest
and wildest imagination, because
the Law now allows and demands that
the few do for the many.

Feel your/our oneness and our togetherness
at this victorious critical moment.
Make no mis-take about any aspect
of what you have just read, and please
re-read this declaration often and do it.

We are grateful in the extreme
because much is riding on You.

4°

OMG,
WE are the Suns of a billion Stars and more!
We are the Song of the Mother/Father God!
We are the Instruments of
the Greatest Love ever given.
We are the ***Peace Commanding Presence.***
Peace: the final frontier.

Remember the training!
You were prepared to look-out for this moment,
when both experiences
(illusion and Truth)
would occur for a duration.

Thank God for God!!
and the "You are that God" training.
Me, I forget it fairly often
and experience the lag.
I need help now and then…to recall.

I must remember to take the time
and "Re-Member" Self, as me
in this most profound moment ever.

I Am God in action.
I Am the being of Light.

5°
Street·Wise

So how would it feel,
to be Ascended and Free, in town?

Imagine or feel this
as a possibility for you:
You are walking down a street
of your home town;
a vibrant Peacefulness pervades.

You hear the subtle sounds of many flowers
opening to the first touch of the Sun's rays.

Your senses come alive and you breathe in
the scent of a billion petals
and the honeyed sweetness they offer
to life passing by.

You see another person
walking in the morning sun
on the other side of the road.
You don't know this one,
but your heart and mind soar at the idea
of this one's enormous identity
and the infinite Circle of Light she carries.

Your Heart feels as if it might explode
with compassion and the kinship it knows
with the one over there
and all that your senses are picking up.

You broadcast and project
heretofore unimaginable glory back
to all life around you…and beyond.

You realize
that the store you have just entered
has manifested for your convenience.
All from an infinite reservoir
of Light Substance.

All this Mind and Feeling
you hold in perpetuity
for all others, known or unknown to you.
And on and on your day goes…

6°
Justice and the Structure of Grace

The Goddess of Liberty
speaks Her Heart and Mind
for our contemplation.
Divine Justice affirms that
Life created in Innocence
will continue to exist *eternally*
in that exquisite Innocence.
Divine Justice is blind to blame
and all other illusions of the human ego.
Rather, It is the embodiment of
Supreme Forgiveness, Mercy,
Transmutation, and Restoration
of the original Innocence
within that aspect of life.

Justice focuses the Healing Forces of God
on a specific goal, undoing any imbalance.
Because the human ego
cannot do the above,
it only finds fault and places blame.

Within the use of the Solar Violet Flame
is the full return of the Holy
and wholly Solar Self:
Love's perfect Presence,
coupled with Mercy.

Mercy invokes affection
toward those who may not deserve it
because of their own misdeeds,
assuming the power to forgive
as the Higher Authority acting.

It entails a kindness
beyond that which fairness demands.
It gives *perpetually and unconditionally*
to Humanity.
It has been given to you,
gentle reader,
known or unknown.

Long ago Humanity and Earth…
would have been vanquished
back into the Light,
had not Mercy been applied
as the ointment that It truly is.

I leave you with the reminder
to Rhythmically invoke –
using the power of the voice
to "shake the ethers,"
bringing about a new inner pattern
of cells, atoms, and electrons
that then outpicture
a new manifestation.

And on and on we go,
creating and freely re-creating
a new Land of Boundless Splendor
and Infinite Light:
New daily life,
together,
on "Main Street."

I Am Group Avatar,
the Heart of Ascended and Free Humanity
and its joyous Peace.

7°

Greetings, Suns of the Sun.
Upon the Land of Boundless Splendor
and Infinite Light we can reside now.
Because the "New Earth" is here, beloved.
It is here, right now.

Just shift your consciousness a little bit
and step onto the New Reality
called "New Earth, New Life."
It is Now, thou Being of Light.

Do not accept appearances as the only Reality.
Choose and choose again.
You are Free and it is Now.
So, no more suffering
and no more poverty consciousness.

From this true place and its space of Being
shall we assist those who are still lagging
for a spell.
You know this already.
You have stepped into the New Light.

Let this be your decree:
I Am a beloved Being of Light.
Then, when your consciousness accepts this Reality,
you just shift your consciousness and you say,
I Am the being of Light.

8°

Perhaps we wish to elaborate on a subject
and Its possibility for anyone to experience:
the Science of being here and there now,
as it applies to the New Earth that is already here.

Let us gather now on Venus,
looking at and hearing
the sights and sounds of the New Earth.
Observe the children bounce
and jump off high structures.
Do you realize your "TV News"
has already captured this?
Already filmed flying people...?
Child painters of unbelievable ability...
Several youngsters in one class
who can read your book
from the other room...!?
and on and on and...

Just see yourself in a farm field
that has gone brown and is stubble.
A few steps away is a fresh beautiful green field
with a narrow ditch of water which divides the fields.
Simply walk over and bless the water
and step over it, into the ***New Earth.***

We all know this is not for everybody *right now,*
but for YOU, who are here NOW...have fun!

9°

From the sweet fragrance of our Love Breath
ever wafting into Humanity's consciousness,
we gather.
The fragrant odor is our remembrance.
We Remember, becoming a "Member"
once again of our **knowingness.**
We do so now, on behalf of the many.

Remember:
**"As I Am raised up (in Consciousness),
so is all life raised up with me."**
Where the few do for the many.

My Beloved Self,
this is the Structure of Grace
that we are becoming…
As in the statement we decreed
from our womb, our own home Sun-system:
for all others.

"I Am the full manifestation of Grace,
the Action of Divine Love
now transforming Humanity."
Feel this, *because I Am the Mother God –*
the act of nurturing, inclusiveness,
mercy, and tolerance –
I naturally attract the Divine Masculine
in my dance of balance.
So I choose to wield the Rod of Power,
the Love Force.

Armed with this re-membering,
with this re-calling,
I now, as One, employ the Power
of the Holy Breath.
Silently, and with deep feeling,
we together can infuse and bring forth
what is needed most.
Being as one Heart, one Vision, one Breath,
in full alignment with all Central Suns
(including the one in your chest
and the one in the Earth's center),
is what is needed most
in this Now Moment.

So, Interstellar Friends, Freedom's Love,
here we go:

***I Am In-breathing and Absorbing
the Perfect Alignment of all Suns
on behalf of Humanity.***

***I Am Expanding and Projecting
the Perfect Alignment of all Suns
in service to Humanity.***

Feel this as your Truth and its Joy,
of this stealthy, cat-like prowess.
We are forcing the inevitable Absolute...
right now.

10°

Beloved Friends, Beloved Masters,
as we (Earth and Us) move forward
in our Solar expression,
Suns of the Sun and Portals of Infinite Light,
the activity of Sacred Breathing
has become evermore useful and poignant.

*We realize that we work
from the realm of Cause alone,*
knowing that the effects will unfold perfectly.
We work absolutely Free
of any time and space constraints.
The Power we wield is also
Absolute and Effectual.

As Cosmic Love Beings
in advanced cutting-edge service to the Light,
we recall the Fundamentals:

See yourself only as a Sun.
The initiation for this highest identity is Love
and all the Qualities of Love
radiating out from you *in all directions*.
The Power of this Love has codes
for all Discernment and Protection, Wisdom, etc.

You are a Sun.
As a Sun, all is under your care –
and **you are not alone.**
And your in-breath and out-breath
are always balanced.

Awareness is mandatory.

An example of our Super Power
in service to Humanity and all Earth's Lifeforce
using Sacred Breath may go like this:

I Am relaxed and poised;
I see, feel, and know that God-Source
is a Huge Great Central Sun.
I know that It replicates Its Self in ceaseless flow.
Which means my Heart Center
is my Central Sun
and every Cell of my Being
is a *Temple of my Central Sun.*

The Light pours into the Heart, then the Chakras...
along my spine...then into all Cells, Atoms, and so on.
I Am a Blazing Sun of enormous complexity...!
A Universe of Galaxies are my organs...
my glands – command centers.

I now let go of all the Truth
of what is going on here
and I simply Am
the Light of this immensity.
Just...AM.

***I Am In-breathing and Absorbing the Light
into the Center of the Earth.***

***I Am Expanding and Blazing the Light
through the Center of this sweet Earth.***

***I Am/We are Divine Directors of Sacred Fire.
I Am Sacred Fire; the whole activity of God.***

(Please repeat the breaths, if you choose.)

11°

Ascended Masters – Cosmic Beings –
Universal Beings that we are:

Walk in the Dignity of the Light
that is pouring through You and out into the World.
Upon hearing certain news of trauma,
hold the Harmony and blaze the Light.

Our Harmony is Our seat of True Power.
The Purest Tao for now is:
to be empty of the affairs of the little self.
One with the Way.
The Way is filled with Cosmic Virtue
with which I desire to Bless the World.
I Am in control
of all energy and vibration
that comes into my World,
wherever I move in interstellar space,
including here on Earth
while inhabiting this body of form.

I Am the Harmony of my Total True Being.
I know myself as an I AM Presence in residence.
I Am a server of Humanity's Ascension to Light.
And I Am here to give.

12°

Being who You are:
As you walk this jeweled planet,
your Radiance becomes and is
a Healing Benediction to the distress
that has passed the way of Earth –
Now the New Earth.

As You pour forth your
Love, Gratitude, and Blessing
to the Beings of the Elements
with constancy,
They will gather around You,
like butterflies in the Sunshine....
Remember this?
I Am the Master of my physical reality.

Breathing Statement:

***I Am In-breathing and Absorbing
the Pink Flame of Thanksgiving
to the Elementals.***

***I Am Expanding and Projecting
the Pink Flame of Thanksgiving
to the Elementals.***

13°
Angels and Gratitude

In Truth and in the Cosmic scheme of Life,
Angels are *the very Breath of God.*
As that, They are the Feeling aspect
of Prime Creator.
They live and operate completely Free
of time and space.
Example: The Christian drama in Judea
was one breath ago.

They are here now to see *this Breath*
through to fruition.

Their assistance is immeasurable
and without limit.

They are needed now,
and they are more than available to You.
Gratitude is by far your greatest invocation
to their immediate assistance.
Your Gratitude is more Powerful
than we could possibly express.
Contemplate this.

Say often,
*Beloved Flame within my Heart,
open, expand, and project
the feeling of Loving Gratitude,
and Bless every part of Life
that enters my Being and World this day.*

14°
Elementals and Gratitude

The Beings of the Elements,
in all their graded orders,
are expecting Us
to consciously and directly
connect with them.

The Original Divine Plan
for Our being here on Earth
is that We would be the Bridge
between Angels and Elementals (Us in the middle),
and co-create ***Limitless Physical Perfection.***
Sounds great.

What happened is the past.
Some have been de-structive to those Beings
in the extreme. <u>Those</u> <u>days</u> <u>are</u> <u>over</u>.
We are here now to re/co-create
what We really want.
*We and the Elementals receive
Celestial Ideas and Feelings
from Angels and Celestials.
Then comes the picture to hold,
with consecration from the Elementals.
We do the footwork* – Form unfolds.

What do I really want?
This is the most powerful question for now.
In it is *who am I?*

***I pour forth all my Love, Gratitude, & Blessing
to the Beings of the Elements
who have assisted me throughout the centuries
and who have hosted me here on Earth!***

15°
Our Immediate Future

And Now,
Our Protection
of the Younger Ones, the Children:
Breathe into the Heart
and create a horizontal connection.

The Youth are here to clean-up
and to re-build the Society.
They are the manifesters of God/Good.

We shall now demand their Freedom:

***No weapon prospers against our Youth.
I Am Their safety acting!***

***I Am the One calling for all the Forces
of Heaven's Light to heed this:
Our demand for the greatest Protection of all,
to enfold all our Youth.***

***I Am the Cosmic Love
and Its unfathomable Power
Protecting the Young!
I Am their clear & present way made manifest,
to the Divine Plan Fulfilled.***

***No weapon prospers against our Youth.
I Am Their safety in Action.***

***And So It Is, And So It Is,
Beloved I Am, I Am, I Am.***

16°
A Brief Recall of all Cycles Converging Here on Earth

As the Great Love of the Hand of Holy Spirit
continues to assimilate all life forms
in, on, and around this Planet,
We – the Disciples of Holy Spirit/Mother God –
receive clearer information into the workings
of this new experience in the Galaxies...

FYI, Your God-Self knows only Perfection and Love,
a part of your Big Self knows both – here and there.
The great alignments are about Five Suns,
each one responsible for aligning
with Its overseer/parent Sun.
All are aligned except the Heart Sun of Humanity,
though very close to Our closest parent,
that being Helios and Vesta –
our local Sun (by whatever name).

So, because this activity
of 7 billion, on a far-out planet
returning to Oneness,
has never been witnessed anywhere,
it is good to chat with and breathe with
any of the several billion Celestials
that are here to assist. Be a direct part
of this awesome Restoration of a Race of Beings.
Bring in something brand new, Ahhh...

Cosmic Holy Spirit is *Mother/Father God
living their Universe into Perfection
through all of us.* Contemplate this!

17°
Adoration's Power

The soft crystalline Pink Flame
and Its clear Pink Light
is the activity of Adoration.
Universally speaking,
if You choose Adoration
as an avenue to Ascend
(and Ascend all life with you),
You would be choosing wisely.
The Soft Pink Light of Love
is the sure short-cut to all other gifts.
It is the projection of "Assurance"
into any part of life
that is seeking the Light,
and It – the Pink –
is the immediate Magnet
to the Blue Fire/Light of Power.

It is the Essence of Holy Spirit
and the Mother God's out-Breath.

The Nature Beings and substance
would gather around
and fill any space available
with Health, Youthfulness,
Beauty, and Well Being for you
when you ask that
your Heart Flame's Love
set them free of discord,
wherever you are.

18°
An Invocation of Remembrance

To my great God Self,
I invoke all of Thy Power
to come out from me here on Earth,
as a flow of Cosmic Love Supreme,
and Be the tangible Presence
of that Great Central Sun's
Magnet's Love of Freedom's flow.
To the many Archangels
and to all graded orders of Angels
who have given their attention to Earthlings,
I Thank You.

To the Many,
Great Elohim and all the Elementals
who have put up with too much already,
I Thank You.
To the Beings within and of the Sun,
all Suns, Central and otherwise,
who have given so much
of their Intelligence (Light)
to the Earth and this system of Worlds,
I Thank You.
I demand a Blessing of Love
go to every Being of Light
who has been giving assistance
to all Humanity and myself,
for so many centuries.
I Am Grateful!
Oh Flame within my Heart,
see to it that this flow of my gratitude
be sustained, forever.
So Be It, Beloved I Am.

19°
Moving Power Points

Dear mobile mechanics,
allow an expanded addition
to your Master identity,
that being a moving Power Point,
a replica of one of the power points
along your mighty Meridians.

Please refresh your memory's knowledge
of what Meridians are–in your body–
to your physical expression.
Along these Sacred Pathways
are specific **points of access**
to and for the greater whole...
like mountains or other access points
along my body. You get the picture.

You are so very important.
For when "creaking" and popping
of my body happens,
that causes worry to the masses,
leading them to medical assistance.

Look at a picture of a Chart of the "I AM,"
or any inspired art diagram
of your True or full identity
(there are a few good ones available).
Because, during this moment
of heaving into "labor,"
you, beloveds,
are the therapists
at my and the masses side.

Just simply choose to:

1) be that great stream of Cosmic Light and

2) ask (choose and direct) it to flow ***directly through your body, out the bottoms of your feet*** *right into the core of Love at the center of the Earth.*

This would be an enormous Blessing from you.

***I Am a Voice of Earth
and you are my Freedom's love
in action.***

***I Am the unbroken flowing wholeness
of my full Solar Identity, assisting.***

20°

Invocation:

Oh thou Infinite Majestic Presence I Am,
Thou Ceaseless Source!
Your Crystal Purity and Your Peace Divine
That I Am, forevermore.
Oh, That I Am, mighty Life,
fill, flood, and charge each one
who gives Thee their Attention.
You are the Inner, Causing the outer.
Cause me to see and know this.
Give me the Feeling of Self!

We forever refuse any more separation,
or any feeling of it ever again!
Keep all of Us charged
with the Feeling of the Truth
of Who We Are!

See to it, oh Self,
that We raise all life
that We contact in any way.
Make each one of Us
a blazing Sun of our Potential...
All life Be Free!

21°

For those who wish to know:
**The greatest Power in the Universe
for your use is Sacred Fire.**
It is what is beating your Heart
at this moment,
and It is what beats every Angel
and Cosmic Being's Heart.
It is the Greatest Intelligence
in all the Universe.
Jesus taught Its use
and demonstrated it many times over.
It is the most hated and feared thing,
by the sinister ones.
Most folk are unknowing of Its presence.

Sacred Fire is the Full Activity of God
and wants to be **called forth
into any constructive action whatsoever.**
Even to remind you to eat and breathe correctly.
That is no joke.

The Sacred Fire within your Heart
and upon *your brow*
(Seven Elohim's Heart Flames)
will leap into Action and fulfill any demand of love,
which you ask or put upon it!
Just ask any Truly Ascended Master,
Cosmic Being, or Angel.

No one makes their Ascension without the use of it.
That is why even the slightest call
to the Heart Consciousness is necessary.
**The Violet Flame is the Keynote aspect
of Sacred Fire for this New Age.**

22°

Hey there, you beloved *Being of Light,*
May We say that your Love is wonderful.
The Sun of God that You are
is exactly *what is* required to set this Earth free.
The next Now Moment is upon us.

Your Constancy
as a *Sun's Presence of Love's Initiations*
is still paramount
to our biggest Heart's Desires fulfilled.

Watch every word.

As you gaze into the mirror,
see yourself radiating great Solar Light.
This is the Truth of your Being,
the Truth of your Solar identity.
As we hold steady in the Light,
many will come to us for solace.
We have become the saving Grace of
"where the few do for the many."

In all things remember this:
I Am the Great Creative Heart of God.

(Note)
In the great original Blueprint for humans on Earth,
the Universal I AM projects a Ray of Its Self
into the womb/Being of the incoming Race of God
(you/us) and expects a rather constant connection
of thought and feeling of creative acts and actions,
to co-create with Angels and Elementals,
a Garden-like Planet of Limitless Physical Perfection.
All within a World of Free-Will...
to become a Sun...and birth more...!

23°
The Activity of Creation

When you choose to bring something into form –
manifested, tangible –
see it inside your head, behind your eyes.
Practice. Really practice.
This works perfectly, by Law.
See the thing when in bed before sleep.
Wake up and be grateful for it.
Feel the love and gratitude
for the Power you will reveal,
the joy you will share,
the accomplishment.
Again, pull the Vision inside
(rather than seeing it out-away).
The feeling of a powerful YES
is a Nova Burst of Power.
"Manifest now, Manifest now, Manifest now."
Why not? Remember, it is the God Power
acting through you, as you, here.
I Am here,
or rather,
Here is I Am.

**By giving Constancy to your Vision
it MUST become physical**
(from wave to particle).

*I Am The Great Creative Heart of God;
what I visualize is real…!*

24°

Beloved Friends,
beloved Star Walkers,
servers of Humanity…

You may recall,
"The Time Is Now."
Or, maybe, "Now Is the Time."
If this rings a bell or two,
you may also recall,
"I choose Peace."
These "wave forms" are inter-atomic
and encoded to go off
when a certain quotient
of the awakening population
is ready for the push they might require.
As Suns of the Sun we fulfill the need.

Humanity must find Comfort…
in order to reverse the momentum
of imbalanced feeling states
at the core of ego's control of daily life.
We know that hunger, shelter,
and basic needs are denied many,
and that many assist along these avenues.

This one Statement
repeated in mantra format
will, by Cause, assist many globally:
"I Choose Peace."
"I Choose Peace."
"I Choose Peace."

Peace and Abundance
are the same Solar or God-Ray.

25º

As Disciples of Holy Spirit,
the best way to bring all revelation and knowing
is to breathe the Flame of Illumination
directly up from your Heart
and ask for its

~

Illuminating Power.

~

On the Out-breath, fill your aura
with its Yellow/Gold Light substance.

Cosmic Love's Illuminating Power
has always been one of the core tools you employ.
Especially here, for this World.
Your God Self is all about:
"I Am the Illumining Power of
Cosmic Love reclaiming this sweet Earth"
as a keynote identity.
The Peace Commanding Presence.
Illumination is Sacred Fire in action
through You and as You,
just by Qualifying your Breath.

Humanity wishes the Peace
that Pure Illumination provides.

For a silent breath, try:

I Am the Breath of Cosmic Peace.

26°

Understanding
"where the few do for the many"
as one of the Great Dispensations
from the Great Central Sun
and its universal "think tank"...

Because Earth and Humanity are the catalyst
for the Ascension of the rest of Creation –
for many Galaxies and beyond.
This is due in part to an act of Compassion,
regarding the assistance that was given
to a group of Souls who needed to further
their evolution quickly...for big reasons.
Earth was made available,
and the loving women of ancient Earth
made the space to allow those Souls
a "Canal" to further their Freedom.
Things have gotten "drawn-out."
Fast-forward to now and you may see
that Prime Creator is more tangibly present
(literally within a mountain,
as Its Central Flame is referred to here).
In other words:
The almost unimaginable is happening
because the unimaginable has already
***"TAKEN PLACE and SPACE" right here
on this little blue mud ball called Earth!***

Remember this one? Seek Wisdom
but get Understanding...a post-grad thing.

***Oh, Great God Self, saturate my Being and
World with the Liquid Harmony of my total
True Being...and Come, Holy Spirit, Come!***

27°

The biggest act of Compassion ever seen
or recorded in the Universes
took place right here on Earth.
All of the Highest Guidance was available
and part of the Plan to assist
a group of souls needing assistance,
who were lagging behind.
Note: It (the Plan) came down to
the women of Earth accepting the Souls
to embody through the ***Womb...***
We must leave it to You to find out more details,
should you wish (*Gnosis and The Law,*
T. S. Papastavro, New Age Study of Humanity's
Purpose, www.1spirit.com/eraofpeace).
Why is this Knowingness so important?
Because the Greatest Love of all
is about to manifest or "make Its Self known"...
and is awakening the Light Workers.
It may have, and will have, emotional upheaval
and letdown, because of the ancient core perception
set around Mother God, Patience, and the Womb.

You see, beloved Masters, Humanity
(which we also are) has not *felt* this Love
for over 14 million years. Add to that,
this LOVE of which we speak has *evolved*
since then – imagine that! Just like The Light,
which you embody, has evolved.

It would be wise to make this a rhythmic Decree:
Great Archangel Michael and All that I Am,
make me ready to embody True Love
and the New Light as the One Presence, I Am.
I ask that all assistance be available to me.

28°
Wild Creativity

A Visualization

Unbridled, unfettered, no more...
The electronic mind-controlling devices acting...

The colorless ones whom we never saw...
are finished. Gone.
The Divine Feminine, demonstrating
Mother God's power of Love's Wisdom...is.
The females of our family on Earth
are also enjoying their embodied piece
as the *Divine Masculine,* perfectly:
The lifestyle of the *Holy Amethyst acting.*
The men, "oddly" enough,
having forgotten how it was a moment ago,
majority wise,
are now focusing on the children's energy fields.
The Divine Masculine ensuring that
the high vibrational, high wattage,
CELESTIAL TRUTHS of Universal Law
are freely flowing,
and played out with
fun-loving, wild creativity!

Still in a bit of awe-struck repose and readiness...
Looking over what is left
and what remains to be loved back
into Freedom's permanence.
We ***all*** find our Self looking into each other's eyes.
Captured by the Divine and its divinity, breathing.
Sighing great tones that are *new to our ears.*

Now listening to the birds
and loving our blessed individuality.
Together we begin,
with our guides, the Children,
the re-make of our daily life...
Steeped in True Freedom – Group Compassion.

A new sort of fun,
the amazing adventure
of World Building.

29°

From the Violet Heart of your Sun
and Its Golden Radiance
do we interface and align with each other.
This accurate and true vision of color
may also be seen as the Golden Heart Center
and Its Violet Radiance.
In the knowing of what shall continue
to "take place" here in this system
and on and around Earth,
it would be helpful to You/I to have and hold
your very own visualization activity
in your Heart and/or your whole body pulsating,
radiating as a light Purple and Gold Sun Presence.

This Help that You would be giving and receiving
is immediately picked up
by your Angels, Teams and Ancestors,
especially the Great Elemental Beings,
who govern your bodies' heath and well being.
Just be Yourself as your own Lilac and Golden Sun,
as one of your new Identities, and see what happens!

**The Violet Fire is now being infused
with the White Fire of Pure Ascension,
hence-Lilac.
These White, Purple, and Gold Suns
are the three MAIN ingredients
of Earth's new expression.**

*I Am a golden Sun's presence of True Love.
I Am the Resurrection and the Life
of the Unity from Above.
And Now as above so below,
in one great Harmonic Show.*

30°

Dear Friends of Freedom's Love,
Co-Servers of the Cosmic Light
to this sweet Earth's Humanity…
We interface with you in the Reality
of your highest identity:
Suns of The Great Central Sun.
You, beloveds, are the Ones
who have stepped into the New Light
and who have done so on behalf of all Humanity.
Knowing the Law of Holy Spirit/Mother God:

*"As I Am raised up,
so is all Life Raised up with Me."*

As Suns of God
you may recall that your Sacred Fire
and Its Light
replicate like ripples on a pond
or better, like laughter in a restaurant.
This simple Law is what the Great Central Suns
(who own this System)
know is the "Ace in the hole"
that wins the vast majority of Humanity
back to Love.
And that Ace is the Open Pure Heart,
which has chosen a different Memory…
Remembering Union as the **Powerful Choice…**
I choose Peace. I remember. The return of AM.
I Am a Global Sun of Divine Love,
The Love Breath of the Almighty.

WE are unstoppable.
*I Am the Mother/Father God,
reclaiming this sweet Earth.*

31°
True Power

Beloved Arisen of Holy Spirit's fullness,
Noble lives of Truth,
On behalf of the next steps
through the new thresholds,
Consider this Invocation to Love's Power
to hold sway…

Oh Beautiful, Infinite, Magic Presence,
of all Creation!
We focus Our mind and feeling
on the New Earth
in all Her Magnificent Splendor.
We Stand, Together as the prominent
Peace Commanding Presence.
Individually "I Am" and collectively
We are the Supreme Creator.
We are the True Power of the Will of Life
(the innocent Elemental Life)
to be Free in the Light of Love, *Now*.

We lovingly ask for all the Powers
of Love's Light available to us
to use our Vehicles,
our Breath, our Voice –
all that we are! –
to Bring forth and Manifest
the Great Command for the Glorious New Age
that every True Prophet and Avatar
ever worked for, right Now on Earth.

We thank You, oh Powers of Light –
all our Friends from above, We Love You.

32°
Imagine This

I Am at the very center of the Universe.
From the standpoint of fundamental Truth,
You are.
Also, from the place of desiring
to be our full Divine Potential
we would utilize this Reality for efficacy.
But consider this as well,
that Earth and all Her codes, etc.,
just so happen to be the *catalyst*
for the Ascension of the rest of Creation.
So, every star system of every galaxy
throughout interstellar space that has been evolving
Free Races has dispatched teams of observers and
"Race Helpers" and others to be here now.
Virtually every aspect of Spiritual
and/or scientific development –
neighbors are here by the millions and millions.
The sky's parking lots are full.
We, HERE, are at the CENTER!

But most important to this one typing is
the Homecoming of fellowship with
the Elemental Beings, Who have conveyed
their indescribable desire to out-picture
the Divine Plan of New Humanity
on New Earth in her New Heavens.
A New Age of *"Limitless Physical Perfection."*
The Age of Holy Spirit, on New Earth.
This refers to the Energy of the AM.

***Am pouring forth all of my Love, Gratitude,
& Blessing, to every Being of the five elements
for their service to me throughout the centuries.***

33°

"AM"
The open Pure Heart
through which flows
the Age of Freedom
for all Humanity.

In this Sacred activity,
I Am empty of the affairs of the little ego.
I Am One with The Way.
The Way is filled with Cosmic Virtue,
with which I desire to Bless the World.

The Perfection of Love in all Its manifestations
is, in short, the activity of Unconditional Love,
Universal Wisdom, and Spiritual Power.

~ ~ ~

*I Am the Perfection of Being
in all activities of my daily life.
The Perfection of thinking, feeling,
acting, and reacting.*

*All former mistakes
were a previous now moment,
and they were Perfect.*

*This is a new now moment,
and it is also Perfect.*

34°

Remember, the Darkness is the Light.

Who you are *is not* Who You Are;
Who You are Is the I AM.

Your reason for being here is:
to Ascend this important Planet.

Be Free of anything less than Love.
Have only one concern: to Bless.

This is *Not* a dress rehearsal;
She is going to burst into a Diamond.

Wear your finest garments
and let the floor show…begin.

35°

For those here who wish to be in
an activity of a service needed now,
here is one that has had a voice of its own
for a spell.
We know it's not for all to participate,
as you all do so much already.
So give yourself a break.
Or…let's harness our Superpower
and do what we can to assist
the **younger generation's** Protection and
Freedom in their awesome task of re-building
the now-incoming new World and its new systems.

------ Here is a Power Template for this Service ------

Thought Form:

A Heart Flame (yours)
is somehow everywhere and within everyone.
This Heart Fire has
a predominantly *Electric Blue Flame,*
enfolding all of the young.

See it first in your region,
then easily see it around your nation
and the continents.

Breathe into this for a few moments,
feeling us breathing together and smiling
as we are the Power.

Please decree with Feeling:

***I Am here and I AM there,
and I Am the only Presence acting there.
I Am the Resurrection and the Life
of our younger generation's
Divine Plan Fulfilled.***

***I am so Grateful
for all assistance to this,
Our prayer.***

36°

We are the Universal I Am
talking back to Its Self.
We are the colorful ones.

We are the intrepid Walkers,
our Career in The Light.
We are the stuff that legends are birthed from.
We are Legendary in the Universes.
We are the Magnet of Love.
We are the Beautiful ones.
Singing Together.
Our Love is so big we put off
what most Beings consider big.
Beloveds, many of you have already
made your Ascension. Your love and kinship
with life in the shadows here has kept you coming
back for more, for more of the others.
Our passion for love has come.

Compassion is Kin-ship;
this knowing brought us back to these sleepy selves.
We said "no thanks" to moving on eons ago,
putting off The Ascension
for those who also have the Flame.

We see only the Flame and Its Light.
We refuse the common definitions of the race mind.
The ever flung, pushy race mind.
I Know who You are and I bow.
To Light only do I bow.

I fold my Wings about my Being
and abide in the Wisdom of The Presence.
I Am, I AM, I Ammm.

...continuing our individual and collective service
to all Life: in, on, and around
this sweet Earth together.

***I Am in-breathing and absorbing
the Cosmic Violet Fire of Freedom's Love.***

***I Am expanding and forwarding
the Cosmic Violet Fire of Freedom's Love.***

37°
Coinage

Dear Co-Servers,
on behalf of all life, Earth's Heart decrees:
It is past time for the Simultaneous collapse
of the unsustainable, exclusive,
debt-based, non-economy,
and it is past time for the rise
of the all inclusive, metal and
culturally based "Total Economy"
to take place and space,
for ALL.
This is no small, small shift–but a *Major Event*.
Most of You have been waiting for this, We know.
The time is Now, folks.
Please know that the criminal web
and its "good 'ol boys"
will be out of the loop
and have very few, if any, hands
on this re-emergence.
This must come to pass now
as a ***signal*** to the rest of life
here and off planet that You/I/We
are of sound mind and Will
to receive the next set of assistances available.
Because Love means **All** in this Act.

So, your patience and willing acceptance
and Peace is mandatory.

Let the Plan of God work out..........

Pause and consider this next service:

Let us Bless all the teachers of our young with our Inner Power.

***I Am the Fire Breath of the Almighty
as I breathe into this True Desire...***

***I Am the Structure of Grace and Cosmic Truth
moving through all classrooms on the globe.
This Fire Breath of God's Blessing
waits for the Perfect time to act.***

38°

Beloved Friends of Freedom's Love,
We wish the exact same thing you wish:
near perfect health, abundant free flowing stuff,
beauty of your own wish,
and the Joyful Peacefulness
that ***Plenty for all*** always brings.
All Freely Given.

We are the Elementals.
We are the One real-time voice
of your very **own** *Body Elemental*
and the Larger, over-lighting Creators
of Nature's systems.

Now get this, if You wish…
We (You and Me)
are living together as "roommates."
For a long time, you have been in your space,
doing what-ever and napping, dear friend.
Ah, but now, you have arisen,
evolved and with vigor!
And you wish to clean-up our space.
So, we–the Ones
who **do** that "manifesting thing"
that you so love–
are "totally down with that!"

To work effectually on *anything you wish,*
use the following:

° Begin with your broadcast of love to us,
  especially your Body Elemental.
  Just adore it...

° Fill yourself with this flowing Violet Fire (!)
  You must see it rise up through you and around
  you. Please ask It to be sustained, and to keep
  you free from returning karmic stuff...

° Ask us, your roommates, to do anything for
  you, like reverse the aging-lie, or bring you
  a few perfect diamonds or some gold, or how
  about give noticeable vitality/youth?

° Pick 1 or 2 things and stick with a clear picture
  of you and/or it, and *Feel.* Then look out...!

***What I see and accept for myself,
I accept for all other children of Love.***

39°

Well, my beloved Self,
friends of Freedom's Love to the Earth,
I Am That I Am.
As it is,
I Am in you and you are in me.
Together I Am, I AM Earth's Victory.
Feeling Our Smile broaden
is indicative of the Harmony of the Truth,
which looks for inclusiveness.

Our mission now is clear:
Cause as much space for Holy Spirit
and Her "River of Love made manifest"
to buoy up as many as possible
to receive what they really want.
Or, to overwhelm the rather slumbering ones
(our family, our self...)
with so much dazzling Light of Freedom
that they call to and allow
their own Heart's Throne Room
to transmute and catapult the self
into Our Self's Reality,
which is the Open Heart of Prime Creator,
Present, as you, right now.

***I Am the Mother/Father God,
allowing Cause to affect the Whole.***

I AM the Global upswing.

40°

For flowing prosperity, simply or greatly
begin using and enjoying a very expansive mind.
Just contemplate a really expansive mind
and you will feel the Truth revealed here.

The Healing energies that flow through You
are palpable and present.
You should harness them
by consciously directing them.

Jesus/Yeshua qualified his hands as Suns,
Suns of Healing Love.
He saw them as blazing Suns
of any color and Quality he wished to use.
And he chose a very expanded mindset.
It just works. Always.

Mother Mary – the part that was Yeshua's mother –
held the mindset for His Immaculate Concept,
as She does now for all Humanity and the Earth.

***I Am the Immaculate Concept
of my own Perfection.***

***I ask for all the Divine Cosmic Assistance
that is open to me – Assist.
I Am Grateful.***

As many may know,
Mother Mary and Earth are merged as One
and Jesus is admiral-commander
of the great intergalactic Mother-ship
called "New Jerusalem."
Both are vast and enormous Consciousness.

41°

Oh Life, Oh Light, Oh Love Divine,
Animating Principle of Life!
Every pulse and every wiggle
is your Breath breathing.
Reveal the Plan and uncloak the Hosts!

Remember: A Sun is the greatest expression
that we are aware of.
Suns call all other Creator Beings into action.
They are the Mother/Fathers
of mother/fathers throughout...

Who You are is a Sun of the Sun of the Sun.
Now is the time for (everything) each one to hold
the Harmony of our True Being.
The seat of our True Power is
Harmony of the feeling body.

Any Sun God will tell you:
When you choose to hold the Harmony
while planets shift,
races experience chaos and old worlds collapse...
yet you hold the Peace in mind and bodies.
You instantly become a Sun God in action
and are protected, communed with,
and upheld in ways inexplicable.

The Way to become a Sun and stay a Sun
is to Visualize yourself as a Sun always.
Let your heart area be the birth center
and let your intuitive imagination fly and go.
Watch how immediate is the response.

The "only" initiation for remaining a Sun
to and for all other life, is Love.
Loving freely in all directions…
Also called the infinite flexibility of Divine Love.
Unshakable Harmony.

42°

Thou delightful majestic Presence I Am.
Thou ceaseless stream!
Infinite and available,
both manifest and unmanifest.
I am in Thee. Thou art in Me.
I Am, I AM, Earth's Victory
in Freedom's Light of Love.

Being Who We are
We interact as One,
servers of Cosmic Love.
Remember the seven levels or spheres
of Consciousness/Placement that wrap this Planet?
One of the higher levels is Joy (and other Qualities).
Her Color is a Peachy/Pink
(not in the accepted "spectrum").
Please consider the following:

Imagine *when you choose **Joy***
as *the motor of the day,*
to be one of your practical helpful tools
that assists everyone you contact....
Throughout the coming days,
as you qualify this Wisdom,
be the space between the drama and sorrows
that are likely to show up in your world,
coupled with the Peace of your Sun Presence
that you have chosen as your Identity,
and Joy being your demand of Self.
What assistance you will be giving
to my beloved Self out there,
Who will surely be wanting it....I Am.

43°

Oh great Cosmic Light,
descend in a blaze of Glory
and set all who are Yours free!
I demand the Cosmic Flame
of Transfiguring Divine Love
expand in all Human Hearts like a grass fire
until all make a clear decision
as to where they wish to go.

Practice breathing this moment,
as the One Heart of a True Desire, to Love.
This is an ancient unknown Love
from the Sun beyond the Sun beyond the Sun;
breathing…relaxed poise…Together now.

A Decree:

From the active still-point within my heart
I invoke the greatest Light
of the greatest Love of All,
and its Clarity of Mind
to expand through every man, woman,
and child in my neighborhood this day.

I Am a Sun, my Love Its Light.
All else rolls back; Earth is free of fright.

44°
Sacred Fire

Friends, ***every day*** remember
and recall the Sacred Fire.
This above all things is the great gift
from on High/God Source
designed for your use
*to keep you free from your own returning
karmic energies seeking redemption.*
If you do not have a comprehensive grasp
on *Sacred Fire,*
just know that **It is beating your heart.**

But the True Law requires
the one needing protection and assistance
to make the call for it to come forward.

I tell You, friend,
not one of the Masters you call upon
made their Freedom without the use
of the Sacred Fire.
It is the **simple, truest help.**

***My Great God Self,
enfold all of my bodies
and every cell of my being
in all activities
of the Sacred Fire's Assistance available!***

***I Am Sacred Fire,
the whole activity of God I AM
and I Am Grateful.***

The reason we say *Sacred Fire*
is the whole activity of Prime Creator
is that It holds and demonstrates
all the Energy, Matter, and Intelligence,
and It is completely free of any limitation
(time or space) to create anything, anywhere.
The Human Race and the atmosphere that
surrounds us is so charged with
limitation-like feelings that we
generally have a hard time proving it.
Though look at a human embryo heart center,
and…(on and on).

It is that Sacred Fire
that calls in, initiates, and ignites
the heretofore unexplained manifestation
of lungs, kidneys, stomach, and eyes.
Let alone the ability to chew, talk,
and write at the same time!

45°

Glowing Suns of Love's authority:
As we commune oftentimes
in groanings that cannot be uttered,
it is perhaps with bated breath
that we await the first breaths
of the entirely New Cosmic Reality,
which is now in waiting.

Beloveds,
Your Supremacy is the ointment necessary
for the common folks' ability to accept
what is best described as:

A woman going in for childbirth
and not only having a different species of child
but the mother transforms and checks out
as a beautiful ET of some sort,
not ever seen before,
with TV cameras covering it all!

You, precious Crystal Gems,
are the *Ace in the Whole*
for the soothing required in the moment.

I Am my Foundation of Love of the World
and I Am the Moment of the Power
of Love's Transfiguring Grace
as the only Show on Earth.

Thus we have
the Unbroken Flowing Wholeness
of the Great Host, as Us.
And the younger folk can manifest
the brand new society with your blessing.

46°

We who are Love's Patience
are relentless toward the goal.

It has always been our Way to gather in "class"
to recall the fundamentals, together,
as a team in service.

First we acknowledge that we,
Masters, chose to come.
Then we acknowledge our absolute responsibility
for every Electron given for our use:
Energy, Vibration, Consciousness, and Creation.
Then our motto:
To know, to dare, to do, and to be Silent.

The "step" we are taking is pioneering
or "catapulting" the race and planet
into a ***Solar Being.***
Just like Jesus demonstrated
40 days after he exited the tomb, so,
**"Greater things shall you all do
than I have done."**

In short, if You were to intend and to hold
the Vision of the Light (being given to you)
entering your crown
and flowing directly through your body
and *out the bottoms of your feet*
right into the Core of Love
at the center of this sweet Earth,
You would be fulfilling and Being
the greatest of Blessings, to all.

47°
Crystal Pyramid

You, **the I Am,**
Divine Instruments of Spiritual Freedom
to this sweet Earth, Suns of Truth,
allow yourself to remember the crystal/diamond,
pyramidal mountain Thought-form...
Breathing easily and deeply...
See yourself as a giving mountain...

You:
water,
protect,
etc. all life.
Plus you rise
above *and* are
a base...You are
a place of Power
and refuge.... **Now,**
just *remember* all the
light pouring into You
from beneath and above...
See a fountain of splendor,
as a Crown cascading down
the four sides of your immense
Presence as brooks and creeks
of beauty...Horizontally right out
from your Base see an endless Ocean
of **Violet Fire** from your Presence that
fills the region of Earth that you protect.
All Elemental life comes to You and all
Celestial, Galactic life pours through You,
the Divine unshakeable Instrument...
of God In Action. In service to Earth.

*Everything that Mount Shasta Is,
the tangible Flame Room
and physical expression
of Mother/Father God on Earth,
That, I Am!*

*I Am the unbroken flowing wholeness
of Fifth Dimensional Consciousness
Manifest for all other life.*

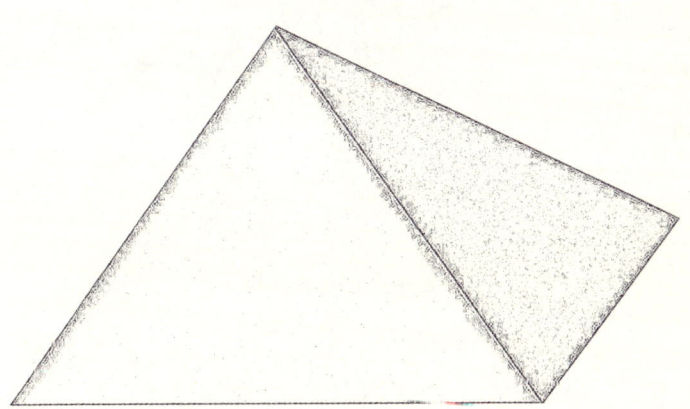

48°

Masters,
our compasses are readying to point South,
a requisite for our and Earth's Ascension.
The North will be dethroned
of its leadership role.

We have a message from the Body Elemental:

"I am the one you contract with to out-picture
the Divine Plan with regards to having
a four-body system on Earth.
I have been your provider.
One of my roles is to coordinate chemical action.

"Here is what you really wish to know
for the Now on Earth.
You wish to bring forward the Divine Blueprint:
Health and Youthfulness.
Three things are all you need to do…

° Know – Feel – that I/We have big Desires
to Transmute and make manifest
your indestructible *Crystal Light Body
of Limitless Physical Perfection…*
Just know this.

° Give spoken Adoration and Gratitude
to Me/Us, your Body Elementals.

° Enfold yourself often in a pillar of Violet Fire,
from beneath your feet,
out four feet or so from your sides,
and well above your head."

***I pour forth all my Love, Gratitude,
and Blessings to my Body Elemental
and to all the Beings of the Elements
for their service to me throughout the
centuries.***

***I Am a living Temple of Violet Fire!
I AM the Perfection
that my Elemental Lifeforce desires.
I Am so Grateful.***

Blessed Stalwarts of Love's Perfection,
You who enact the Law of
where the few do for the many,
I bow before your great Light of Love,
embodied here as Cosmic Suns.

In our Vision of Humanity's Enlightenment
on Ascended Earth, the great Elohim,
which are the highest graded order of Elementals
and other Cosmic Beings,
are *sounding* the picture and feeling
of Love's Power to be utilized at this moment.
Many of you, gentle readers,
already know this so well.

For ourselves who wish to:

Your Heart Flame is an exact replica
of Prime Creator's creative Center,
often called Love (pink),
Wisdom (yellow-gold),
and Power (Blue).
Acknowledged in that order,
because Love is first.

The Blue is the "Electric Daddy,"
of Masculine.
It is energizing Power.

The Pink is the Mother's nurturing river.
It is Magnetic Love.

The Yellow-Gold Flame and its Sun
is the Solar Christ, the mature Child.

Consider and contemplate
the Power aspect first, for the Now.

***I Am the Power of Love's Illumination,
forcing Humanity awake.***

***I Am the Power of Love, as the Solar Christ.
The miracle Magnet.***

50°

We, the ones who are of "Privileged Embodiment"
here on the hottest piece of real estate
in all the Galaxies, are truly privileged.

Recalling one of the great Laws of Life:
Consciousness Dictates Reality.
There is a large aspect of ourselves
who lives and flourishes under the surface.
There are more than a few races/varieties
who have been with us for centuries.
Most of you, gentle readers, are aware of this.

What is poignant for us now
is to use the great Law of Love from our hearts
and to send our acceptance to those mentioned.
Who, by the way, have held Harmony and Vision
for Earth's Purity of atmosphere,
surface, and safety, for eons.

I remind myself:
The Divine Plan for Earth is…
***the full Re-Unification of all life
on the surface of Earth.***

For those who may feel this part of the Plan calling,
just allow your Attention to go to them,
often called Middle Earth
or the Agartha Cities of Light,
and they (the Light) will register your Feeling.
Now, especially the Children of those centers
will direct their emotion and joy to you
in Unity of purpose.

51°

Dear Friends, as Freedom's Flame
continues to overwhelm ego's fears,
the Resurrection Flame and Its
sure momentum will assist you,
and through you, as you use It, all other life.

Here are a few powerful Solar/Sun Being
Resurrection Decrees:

*I Am the Resurrection and the Life,
of Infinite Gratitude for all the Blessings
Life has bestowed upon me.*

*I Am the Resurrection and the Life,
of every good and perfect thing I need
in my service to Life,
including money and supply.*

*I Am the Resurrection and the Life,
of Perfect Health, Eternal Youthfulness
and Well Being.*

*I Am the Resurrection and the Life,
of "Limitless Physical Perfection" on Earth.*

*I Am the Resurrection and the Life,
of my full Solar Reality,
now walking the Earth.*

*And as I Am raised up,
so is all life Raised up with me.
And God's light is fully free on Earth.*

52°

Great Presence that You are,
I speak in sequestered space with you,
and through you to the many.
I Am the Self that is Free.
You have chosen Freedom too.
For the many here, like you,
have not known True Freedom as a family,
the planet included, for far too long now.
Those expressing True Freedom here
have been hunted down and snuffed out for eons.
Blah, blah... Now, here we are and we –
the Earth Herself and people – are free,
even though the last lingering piles
of conflict are still appearing.
Know this for us!

Give Great Honor to the Younger Generation.
They are to manifest your wildest,
most totally Free, Field of Dreams,
with Us or without Us.

Never forget Who You really are – God.

53°

Great host of Light, Earth-side,
you who are aware of our absolute Oneness
and the direct connection that you have
with us/Self on the other-side,
it would be most fun and perfect
when we establish the profound
and simple activity mentioned prior,
when you here take that moment and declare:

*I demand my outer self here on Earth
be established as a living portal
of any and all of the Cosmic Light
of the Cosmic Love or whatever assistance
my God Self, I Am, wishes to give here.
Come and pour that assistance
right through me now,
to all Elemental life that my expanded
aura can possibly touch this day.
So Be It, and I thank You.*

We will overwhelm any plan or acts
adverse to God's Love constantly.

54°

Mighty Forces and fields of Love that we are,
in the setup of any act of creativity
the mental body should move
with bright vibrancy:
the activity of the Higher Mind.
As we breathe on that,
the Air and atmosphere
set up the environment
that is instantly responsive to any Feelings...
We would remember that
any act of breathing brings a focus
of your Heart's Sacred Fire activity.
As masters of creation –
on behalf of all other life –
we know what to do.

We could say, "We water this planting."

Consider:

I Am a being of Flame and I AM It's Light.

I Am the Wisdom, governing all that manifests.

I Am the sustaining Power of every constructive thing I Desire.

55°

Beloved people of Earth, I Am That I AM,
that all here have so petitioned
at some time or another for assistance,
call me what you wish.
I wish to call you **Self.**
For those who know themselves as Me/I Am
they know that it is the *Feeling*
that is your *knowing.*
So, I, as *you,* wish for that Feeling
to be transferred/given to the common folk.

Whatever your path of service or groups of Praise
you share *in common circles* and enjoy,
it is for you to *be aware* that I Am coming
to find that Feeling and receive
my awaited Freedom also.
It is also for you to know, beloveds, that I AM
the common Folk, the regular, confused,
weighted-down people.
As you hold true to the Immaculate Concept
of your service, you will Feel this hoped for
Transference – You to Me.

Compassion is
I Am here and I Am there.

This is a flawless service.

56°

Profound awe goes before this Voice to you here.
To Light only do I bow.
And bow I do, before Thee.
I Am called the Goddess of Liberty.
I am known as Mother of the Violet Fire
of Freedom's Love to the Earth.

Briefly, I must remind you, Self, that the Violet Fire
has been used throughout the Galaxies
for assorted reasons. Specific to Earth,
to Liberate a Race of God Beings and Elementals
dominated by ego enthronement for far too long.
Our Saint Germain is the Violet Fire...
I, as Mother, wish to dance with the Electric Power
of the Masculine aspect of Gaia through you.

Suffice it to say, your determined,
rhythmic application of
The Only Thing That Could Set You Free
is needed to keep your chosen Vision and Hopes
of the complex Divine Plan in Order.
This, my love, you already do.
I just need a little more rhythmic, Joyful Application.

Also, remember that
Forgiveness is the Hub of the Universe.

I Am the Violet Fire in Action
Now and for all Eternity.

I Am the entirely New Cosmic Reality
now anchored and emerging
through all life on Earth.
So Grateful, I Am.

57°

We speak as One, and I Am there,
which is here: Cohesive and Free.
To be the much needed Illumination
you must assist other life.
Contemplate this:
The Threefold Flame in my Heart
is the All of God…literally.
What is underway is the full return of
The Feminine Ray and the balanced
"Age of Spiritual Freedom" made Manifest.

Illumination must also be underway,
rather constantly,
in order for Her Qualities to be infused
as Natural in the bigger decisions
and actions of daily Life.
For example:
In the old world of agriculture,
certain crops that are grown
are *part* of an ego, separated from balance in form.
Example: too much coffee, sugar, or plastics,
which are big things in our lives,
require The Power of Love's Illumination
to change Harmoniously.
Harmony, beloveds, is your seat of True Power,
and Illumination of the individual
quickly fills the collective.

Best to breathe the Center Flame of Illumination
right up, directly from your Heart,
Its Sunshine, Golden Yellow substance.

***I Am the Fire Breath of the Almighty,
the Illumination for all.***

58°
Able Assistance

Considering the portal or fountain
of the Greatest Light of all
(Ascended Masters, Cosmic Beings, etc.)
that is trying to pour into Humanity
for reasons that are obvious...

...Grasp the simplicity of the Law.
Every day ask your own God Self
and The Greater Light,
the Greatest Light of the greatest Love of all,
to pour through you and charge
your ever-expanding aura to at least
a one mile (2 km) radius in every direction,
raising every person, place, condition,
and thing which your aura contacts
into greater Perfection
just because You have passed its way.

When You do this with your determination,
then You have become the answer
to our quest as to *how* we will reach
the unawakened folks
and replenish Nature directly.
We tell you,
only through your bodies
is this possible.
It is so.

59°
Our Animals

Today in a small clearing
in your southern hemisphere,
a profound hush of Peace Divine
alerts all the gentle dwellers
of the surrounding forest.
They have been waiting for this austere moment
of inevitable Re-Union...
as the welcoming door of our Crystalline,
Pearly Opal, Sun Ship fully settles...
The Joy – that is only experienced on Earth – fills
us to tears and marries the Peace.
As the chosen group of the little ones
humbly begins to file into the embrace
of our assistance...
(they have always been ours too)
they, the "animals,"
have endured the "onslaught"
for far too long.
This new experience for them
is a bright step in their evolution
that Freedom's Love guarantees all life.
The others sigh their "so long"
as our transport quietly leaves
the palpable print of our emblem.
And the Fire of our hearts
is breathed by them
as they melt away
into their hidden dens and beds.

Am, the clear Pink Ray,
Am, the Mother God,
returned to Earth to stay.

60°

Fellow International Co-Servers,
walking Christs of the Buddha Nature,
From our rooms of Universal Science
and Holo-decks, let us wax for a moment
into post-grad recall, so as to ensure
the knowing of what is manifesting,
True Science and Its Wisdom, or Love's Demand.

° From the Suns of your Origin
the entire replica (hologram) flows
into your tangible presence here,
cascading into every cell (temples),
then outward – through radiance –
creating daily life, i.e., River to Ocean.

° The Divine Plan (Freedom) is to ensure
that the Light of Freedom's Love
be made more than possible
for every single person on Earth.

° The science of it is for a portion
of the free-will population
to choose Truth – choose what we are.

° As our dear Jesus performed,
He became the authority of a Blazing Sun,
attracting and helping others.

° Simple job, post-grads...
Contemplate being a Sun,
every day, for all life.

I Am the Light of the World.
All of the World is within me.
All of the World is Light.

61°

Unshakeable readers,
We have become
a rather coherently connected group
of Conscious Divinity in action.
Individually I know, I Am.
Collectively we are Its Supremacy pervading.
Today the directive is to visualize this, please:

Conscious of the Light flowing
into my head and hands,
I become a greater Sun, instantly.
I direct this Fiery Light to flow
directly out the bottoms of my feet,
into the Heart-Mind of this Earth.
(visualize)

I qualify It to also be used
to cease anything other than
the Divine Plan for Earth,
fulfilled in Peace.

***I Am the Solar Christ
and Buddha Nature
as the only Moment
acting through all Humanity.***

***I Am the Mother/Father God
reclaiming this sweet Earth.***

62°

This much needed service, and our Joy,
is best given through this visualization:

You are sitting there.
Enter into the Regal thought
of your True Being
as a core of White Fire,
a Golden Sun with a soft Pink Aura
(the Violet is already there by momentum).

The Inner White, Golden glow,
and Pink, inviting, projecting.

Now see, really See, the Earth as a White Sun,
a dazzling White Star of Spiritual Freedom,
Her mother-of-pearl Radiance.
Hear, listen to the Song of Happiness
and awe of the people.
Everywhere your thoughts go
you hear the song of Comfort and Joy.
People are doing for "work"
only what they love to do. Hah!
All stuffs are given freely.
The active Union of the expressions
of Angels and Elementals,
now "Bridges" through Humanity.
EARTH!

***I Am the entirely New Cosmic Reality
of Absolute Freedom on Earth.***

63°

Blessings, beloveds, You who are...
*"the Purity of Love formed
and offered through the Cosmos,
to Purify, Transmute, and Bless
all that is not of the Light
back to its original Divine Intent."*

As our ships of Love's Perfect Presence
come ever closer
into your irresistible substance
of clear Pink Light,
We shake hands with You,
the Golden Hu-Being.
Immediately our core of White Fire
expands and superimposes itself.

Now We all get busy
as the White FireBeings,
as our highest identity,
androgynous Doers of the next Step.

We work with the young ones,
who are now revealed
as the Universal Builders
that they really are....
Wild Creativity
is the order of the New Day.
Everything is revealed,
Tangible.

64°

Friends and Masters of Universal Law,
Divine Instruments,
I Am the Voice of Gaia.
It is in Unity Consciousness
that I speak and sit with you for a moment.
When I "crack my knuckles"
or "pop my knee" into place,
the unsustainable aspects
of Humanity's world suffer greatly.
If I need and receive
a shoulder or hip "snap back"
due to a long-standing discord...then catastrophe.
I Am scheduled for
a couple of those appointments
by Order of my Ascension.
What You are "appointed" for
is continual daily upgrades
of greater Unity Consciousness
in active Principle.
For instance,
sending your Love and Blessing
from your Highest Heart, I Am,
to the whole of Nature
and the Beings of the Elements.
Contemplate Coherently Connected
Divine Consciousness
and the Force-field of Holy Spirit, both.

We are moving this planet,
and many wish to stay on board.
I use Mother Mary's
vast Consciousness in Unity,
daily, for all of You.

65°

Oh gentle Masters,
out from many Suns of the Great Sun.
It is you to whom I appeal
on behalf of the many, the clouded.
I Am the Voice of Gaia,
and the focus this day, I ask, is on
the rapid Healing of your neighbor's emotional body,
that which has taken on so many altered,
backward states of being.
That which must come,
into that which will Heal Her is,
***the Sacred Fire Healing Love
of the All of God everywhere.***
Also, it is for You to know now that
the biggest job/event for me to experience is
the return of my axis to the Universal Axis.
This is accomplished only with the assistance of
Great Cosmic Beings of Universal Proportions,
and You, because **You are the Correct Axis,**
which enables me to assume
my next Ascended Orbit,
which Beloved Venus is still holding for me…
the Orbit of Divine Love and my expression,
Freedom.
So, emotionally, Humanity…
We will speak on this another time.

66°

The words "I Am" throttle forward
in every direction,
the Powerhouse of the very Hand of Creator
and/or creation, the Universal,
to accomplish the spoken thought/feeling
of the sender. This you know.
What is Fundamental to you, the sender,
is getting where you really want and wish to go.
Yes?

Meanwhile you, know it or not,
are doing all of this,
in an atmosphere/soup
of throbbing human creation:
though having been greatly purified,
it is pushing to the hilt,
in order to maintain itself.

Here's what works:
"I am sitting or reclining comfortably.
I acknowledge that I'm an extension
of Central Source, That 'I AM.'
Breathing easily, deeply and perfectly,
I smile and give my attention to That I Am.
I tune into my spine, I feel the moving Energies
as they flow along my Meridians of Light.
This creates the matrix
for my wholly Ascended Self to interface,
merge, and assimilate more greatly
this outer self—in the moment and in daily life.
I see with my Mind a steady picture
of a sea of Golden Light,
the Christ Consciousness
of every part of my being."

Now, I choose to just *be with*
this *Golden Being* that I Am.

Because the Law of Love is:
**The outer, slower vibration must relax
and "be still and know, that I Am God."**

How this works is this: Thoughts will come up,
but the real plan here is not to judge yourself *
for not being able to stay "free of thoughts."
The outer mind is a thought-producing machine,
though it *needs a rest.* It needs a break!
Really it does!
It is just that it is not You.
It is only a part of You that is,
or used to be, under your guidance.
As you persevere and continue
*Being with the Sunshine Yellow/Gold Flame
or Sphere of Light that is your cells' aura...*
a great Light *will open up within you.*
Your whole World will see **and** feel it.
I Promise.

* Because, if you're judging yourself,
you are judging the World.
Because, *You are the World, beloved.*

67°
A Voice of Earth

Bless You, dear Friend of God.
I wish to continue with
our communion-subject at hand, which is
Pioneers of Consciousness and
use of the Crystal Pink Flame/Fire.
Always, we acknowledge and apply the first:
Be still and know That I Am God.
Know (if you don't know, look into)
the fact that you have a huge *Causal Body*,
filled with the momentum
of previous accomplishments and experience
in the constructive use of The Laws,
to be used **Right Now** for the big Cosmic Climax
taking place here upon my surface.
It has a will. It comes forth through
acknowledgement and intent to flow.
Then, importantly, the Quiet Stillness –
space between the thoughts.
Its Permanence is Love,
your Attention is the action of your Love.

The Pink Flame is
The Great Cosmic Magnet of Cosmic Love.

You are Divine Directors
and You are Sacred Fire, period.
Command the Sacred Fire as a Cosmic Being
to supersede and superimpose every activity,
coming or going, Human or otherwise.
Direct the Light flowing into You to my core.
I thank you loudly, for your part in this
Victorious flow of Love and Peace.

68°
Papa Earth

Dear Presence of Universal I AM, here.
Due to our established Crystal Pink Fire,
the open Heart, we have pulled My complement
into the Dance of our Communion...
I Am the Electro Energy,
Daddy part of this Voice of Gaia.
You who know the Law know that for "Hu-Beings,"
Love's permanence must *be*.
I speak now with You as graduates.

What I "need" of You – on behalf of all other life –
is your Highest Mind, your very expanded Mind.
When you choose to "get all up in your head" with,
let's say, stepping out of a boat
and walking to shore,
you would be experiencing the Miracle Mind.
Beloved, if you were to see Humanity clearly
in your head, in general Peacefulness
during this "teething" period of the changes,
it is your "sold-out" intent to hold the Vision
that will *ensure* that you, beloved,
will breathe, dine, and sleep in usefulness
to the Law of Harmony.
And it is the flow of your Causal Body,
which is our Certain Victory of everything,
that the Open Pure Heart of God in action wants.

***AM the manifestations of my Crystal Vision
for all included.***

***AM the matrix, of Sacred Flames.
I Am as the all of God.***

69°

Outrageously Blessed are we
whom life has called to be a working part
of you and yours–"the Away Team."
I Am the one voice of the 12 Elohim.
We have each of our Heart's Flames
anchored and ablaze around your head as
"The Crown of the Mighty 12."
As "Papa Gaia" asked
for your sustained Crystal Vision,
we wish for you to know more.
Our actual Heart Flames are present
around your brain structure,
to ensure that the Builders of systems of Worlds
and their Eco systems of Nature
are a continual working Presence *with* you.
Like all attributes,
all we require is your acknowledgment.

So breathe into your Heart deeply
and let Her Fire rise up through your neck
and up into your head,
inflating it with the Heart of God within you.
There you are. Now allow one,
or as many Colors of Life as You can Visualize,
to create a full Crown of Flame.
See this for a moment. Looking up,
feel the River of Light flowing into your crown.
Intend that stream to flow directly
through your body and out the bottoms of your feet
right into the core Palace Room
at the Center of *this sweet Earth...*
Snap back to this Vision throughout the day.
Know this: ***I Am the Cosmic Being
to this Planet's Freedom in the Light.***

70°

You who are the Doctors of Love
and structures of Grace,
I, the Angel of Unity (Consciousness),
Stand in your bodies (as you),
that which has been and that which **is** New.
One is still given much attention,
the other is rooted and pulled out of the soil.
Its stem and primary leaves
are turning upward, fully erect,
Standing in the Light.
Consider the New Earth as a Green field
which you see while standing in a plowed,
dirt field of old Earth
that many are walking upon.
The freshly green and tall grass
is just over a little ditch of flowing water,
waiting for you, any and all, to step into it.

I tell You, beloveds,
the New Earth and New Humanity
are already here!
It is Now, Beloveds.
Already flourishing right in front of or beneath you.
Consider the Fundamentals of any World Religion
and the Avatar (a person, mind you)
who demonstrated it.
Add to that the Earth's Evolution now.
And you may be Enlightened to this Truth for you.

I Am the Entirely New Reality
of Earth's Now Moment, felt by me.

71°

Within the context of Unity Consciousness
and the Great Divine Plan's absolutes,
it is for you to know that
the Middle Earth Civilizations must re-unite
with the surface folk and with daily life.
How can it be otherwise if we are
to live here free of denial?

For you see, the raising of our New Family,
of Love and Love alone, inevitably includes
a large percentage of population that may
still be leery of what Unity may bring.

Hear us. A part of the first day
of the newly birthed/awakened
is the need for "milk."
This "milk" for *some* will be
the real-time acceptance
of the Inner Earth folks' re-emergence.
Do you see?
We do not say it will be their first breath
or their first steps, but the nutrition that is needed.

Now, You are the One Great Presence
that says, I AM. Please know that
I AM Unity Consciousness
is the adventure of a lifetime!
The Violet Fire of Freedom's Love
and your Heart Flame carries it all.

Beloved Flame within my Heart,
Expand and set me Free.
And Violet Flame,
keep me Free!

72°

Cherished Children of the Sun,
who are also parents of a civilization,
an I AM Race,
about to take command of all aspects
of the rebuilding of,
then the recreating of,
then the flourishing of,
what is Now,
and also is the Light.

You, Beloveds, will be the Light
that will be seen from distant Galaxies
upon a star burst that will be called
The Star of Spiritual Freedom.

I Am a Being of the Rose Pink Flame.
I AM the return of the Mother God
and this Earth I do Claim.

73°
Earth Speaks of a Love

Friends of Solar Being,
I Hope to be as Inclusive as Life's magic will bring
to all who may read this subject.
Let us turn our Love through our attention
to the gift of The Violet Flame
and what it has allowed for my continuance.
Long ago all "races" of humanity
would have been removed from my surface
and my Planet been dissolved, back into the ethers…
were it not for the individual Consciousness
of the One we call Saint Germain.
His determination to see and experience
Humanity's Holy Evolution unto her Freedom
was heretofore never before witnessed in Creation.
He even laid down his Crown
of garnered, magnificent jewels,
as the balance required by the Councils
for an extension to be given to Humanity.
This is the Quality of *Sun God Patience,*
which, mind you, can be withdrawn
on behalf of the Freedom of the whole.

No other being loves you, Humanity,
as much as the Mighty Saint Germain.
Of course, his action could not have come
without the (Love) actions of all the other Avatars
who came (acted) before This King of Love's tenacity.
Love alone has won.

> *We love you, Saint Germain.*
> *We love your Violet Flame.*
> *We Love your Sacred Name,*
> *Beloved Saint Germain.*

74°
The Plan

Co-Servers, continuing our contemplation
of certain truths and The Truth,
allow yourself a moment of zero time.
Be still and feel the energies of the AM,
the Master Presence. AM, a part of a great plan
to set a planet and Her Beings free.
Just feel the happy inclusion.

The following is True…
There is, and you are part of,
a great and complex Divine Plan
that is the greatest story known in the Galaxies.
You are in the leading roles.
Imagine an out-of-control prison,
and a plan, which entailed you getting arrested and
becoming a convict – repeatedly, over and over –
and not knowing who in the population
is part of the ***Freedom Team,*** and who is not.
Now feel as if this is True for you.
The Plan is to become a literal Sun through intent
and the desire to love all life free.
It would entail having a group of beings
show up as children who are already SUNS.
They have no process to go through.
These are the ones who just ***DO***
(manifest everything).
BUT, a new and forgotten Love of such magnitude
that It must be prepared for
or else it won't flourish, must be in Place and Space.
Contemplate the Power of "a New Love."

This is the Place where we are.
So, heal all emotional wounds ASAP.

75°

Temples of Sacred Fire, and Our Oneness.
We are the Gathering of
the New Human upon New Earth.
With regards to the truth of the above greeting,
I wish for us to recall the Memory of the Love Ray
and a few of Its performances on Earth.
It was Love and Love alone...
that brought Sanat Kumara out of His home.
He persevered for over four million years
and endured the slaughters of his temple of Love
by human ego choices.
And Quan Yin, who put off going forward
into the greater bliss after gaining Her Freedom,
because her loved ones (human beings)
were still in the shadows.
And Jesus, who endured rejection
and family persecution
that only Love and Its Permanence could consume.

This all comes forth now to be the Memory
that we must demand be the Truth,
of the next Now Moment for daily life everywhere.
Because those who are the sinister ones are betting
on our old fears, within the *cellular memory,*
of the collapse of former Golden Ages (Freedom),
and they are preparing – by will –
to play that card again.
We know this and **we Remember.**
We choose Peace. I Am, I Am.

I Am the Love that knows no opposite,
I Am Its Constancy, acting.
I Am the Open Pure Heart
through which flows the Memory of Truth for all.

76°

Well, my beloved self, I Am Earth.
Today you may feel much happening
within the structure of your bodies,
because much is being moved
and corrected in areas of my body.
Love allows for this.
As you know,
You have become the Divine Instrument
of the Dispensation
that holds, can see, and actualizes
the New Age of Spiritual Freedom.
The full return of the Divine Feminine
and the *fun* of the transformation
of the masculine into *the Divine Masculine*.
The rebuilding of my household.
During this rebuilding, now underway,
be aware that there are those
who hate the Divine Mother still.
All is in Order
and this is about finishing
within a realm of Free Will, Choice,
and Right-use-ness (Righteousness)
of what manifests.
So, it is said,
let us open our open Hearts a little bit more.
Then even more.
And your Gratitude is everything.

I Am the Voice of Gaia
and I am so grateful for
your Power of Healing.

I AM the Resurrection and the Life
of Humanity's Divine Life on Earth.

77°

Imagine, if you will, the Truth of Your Being.

Imagine that you can have anything you want,
when You ask from your Heart.

Imagine being unafraid of Your Power,
and using it often!

Great God Self,
Oh Mighty I Am, which I am,
Come forth!

Angels of the Cosmic Love Fire,
Fill and flow through me this day.

I ask that all the gifts
imprinted upon my brain structure
be revealed now.

As one with all life,
I Demand the protection
of our younger folk sustained.

I Am the Heart of God
asking these Demands,
for the Highest Good of all.

78°

My beloved Self, I love You.
I so enjoy our rhythm of breath
and the Sacred Communion it has established.
For as you know so well,
the homecoming back to Love
and the New Human of the New Age is,
in a word, all about Communion.
This refers to one of the Laws of Life that states:
**Where your attention is,
and what you meditate upon,
You become.**
As a voice of Gaia,
I wish for more of you to meditate
or return your focused thought
to the Golden Sun Presence
(the Golden person) ***actuality***
that the great recent "Saviors" and Avatars
(which ***You are*** in this Now) advised.
Because the Golden Substance of the All –
the Christ consciousness –
has the Peace and Abundance and Magnetism
and is the Great Solar Quiet
of Cosmic Peace Divine
that is now and will be
the commodity of all commodities,
that *those who you are here to serve* require.

***I Am a Golden Sun's Presence
of Cosmic Peace Divine.
I Am everything
and all Humanity needs
at this time.***

79°

On this planet, a new type of human has arisen
and the Sun in our heavens is a new person(s).
This is a literal, scientific statement.
Medical science is aware of the first, and most
of the world of astronomy is aware of the latter.
Isn't it glorious that we are seeing the inevitable
on all fronts,
including the frontline science
and spiritual doers converging?
This is one major facet of the gem
called "zero point."
My adopted vision is,
when the cover
of Popular Mechanics magazine
is showing us the same
as New Age or Nexus magazine,
it must be coming from everywhere!

Regarding the "Convergence,"
what is the "thing"
that allows and matters most,
to assure that the inter-celestial experience
will unfold?
You know it – happy, peaceful Harmony.
If there is a day when I am out of Harmony
and upset – No worries!
We Are/I AM, our True Identity,
here as individual and as group.

The group is holding the Harmony for you – the One.
This scientific/spiritual Truth/Law
could very well be a usable or important piece
to have and to hold.

So, as an individual,
I have chosen the Ascension (Peace),
and as a group,
I have chosen the Ascension.
How it works is by the Law of One.
At times of great converging cycles,
the womb energies as well as the outer realities
reflect the Hologram/Whole
as individual time and space collapse.
Solo becomes collective...

Our I Am is everything.

I Am empty of the affairs of the little ego.
I Am the Harmony of my total True Being.
Thank God for God.

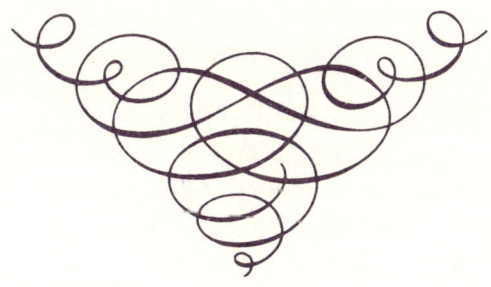

80°

World Servers,
through that great Love that you so Love,
I, Micah, the Angel of Unity,
convey from your Earth/Gaia
the Vision She is holding today
for this Mystic Moment of change.
She wishes those who can,
to see and feel the young ones of the Middle Earth,
(Telos, and the Agartha network, etc.)
or even to hear them.
They, of the Middle/Hollow Earth – because
they are keenly aware of the next Now moment
of a *transition walk* into a New Reality – have bright
vibrant visualizations and powerful desires
of being in and about people's daily life.
Right now, beloveds.
She asks you to actualize any vision
and feeling you would,
of interacting with a group of folks
or the wee (fairy) kingdom
who just suddenly appear.

Think about an unimaginable World
of all kinds of formerly hidden
and subterraneous humans, ET's,
and more Celestial folks,
all having a prosperous time
with the formerly "leave us alone" humans
right down on Main Street.
At the Pubs.

81°

Blessings, beloveds,
together Standing in the Light, indeed.
Keep your attention on the Power of God,
the Power of Prime Creator within You.
Focus on the Power of Prime Creator AS You.
Just keep returning to this feeling all day.
Remember the Power of Bright Crystal Vision.
As God in action,
you may – we may – "tip the "scales"
and override and supersede
the altered timelines (possible scenarios) that
we, who are afraid, are now energizing.

Remember your power to visualize
is God's Power acting. Yes?
Know **that** first...

Let's apply the Law together now
and really see *the local region where you live,*
the school, the market, the park...
all in Harmony,
emitting this astounding Light.
Thou Art God.

82°

Cosmic Love is the full experience
of Source within a certain domain
and has not been known by the masses
(who we are here to serve) for far too long.
Cosmic Love is always complete manifestation as…
I Am a Sun of full Divine Manifestation.
This affirmation IS what is the news
and IS what is "happening."
Even though ticket holders differ
as to where the next stop will be,
all stops are temporary
because all life Ascends.
Yes?

This Sun of full Divine Manifestation
now is occurring on a global scale.

Cosmic Love is the full measure
of Mercy and Forgiveness
ensuring that "all" energies are included
in this final Ascension of Earth
into her next awaited step.
This Mercy and Compassion
passes the understanding of the outer mind
and is a principle Foundation
of the *Mother God re-balancing this World.*

***I Am Divine Love
and I Am what is actually happening Here.***

83°

Friends of Life and all its expressions,
returning our attention
to the use of our Power,
of Love's Illumination
and its requirement.
We would be of enormous service to self,
to touch upon this use of the Law of One,
through a simple but far-reaching Visualization...

The Electric Blue Light
of fatherly, energizing, Causal power
pours into my upper body
through my open crown.

The soft Pink, motherly, magnetizing Light/power
fountains up into my lower abdomen
through my open feet.

A Golden Sun Presence
(of New Humanity) is created,
becoming my predominant figure and feeling.
Visualize and feel this.

We thank you with all our hearts,
for what you visualize is real.

As I am raised up as a Sun,
all life is raised up with me.
It is so.

84°
Spiritual Power

Eternal Friends,
through humanity's (our) **assured anchor
into Love and the steady flow of Illumination**
(of a Plan) revealing all things,
we naturally step into the focus of Power.
Love's Illumination had to be fully in place.
Spiritual Power is where the fun begins
to take on the Feelings of True Desires.
For instance,
an aligned use of Power may be to commit
to being a constant radiation,
magnet, and Blessing,
to the Beings of the Elements or Angels.
This sort of rhythm creates Purity,
which is another subject altogether.
Though realize this:
Those who do not love life or children
use Power and get what they want
manifested, temporarily.

Spiritual Power,
for the advanced I AM Beings,
is to wield Sacred Fire.
Those who do, use Spiritual Freedom
in Universal Service right here
for the Highest and most Good.

I Am the Resurrection and the Life
of Limitless Physical Perfection on Earth.
I hold perfect pictures, often.

85°
Universal Wisdom

Gentle readers, it was You
who chose to reach ever higher,
as a creator God-being (v.),
coming into deep density.
We were and are given privilege and support.
A part of Wisdom is the knowing/feeling
that within me is (I Am)
the localized presence of The Big One.
It is on this Truth we might contemplate:
Wisdom for the whole Moment is certain,
affirming that The River of Life pours in.
The Ocean of Life is within.
Divine creation ensues.
Or, "I Am the Light of the World.
All of the World is within me.
All of the World is Light."

Consider also
Knowing this Truth,
that I Am God being (active).
Wisdom (for all) is
the right use of whatever manifests.

In short,
the Wise one is the one who loves.
Thou art God.

86°

As the intensity of Now expands
and anchors ever greater flow,
keep the memory of "All Life Ascends" close to you.
Ascension is the foundation of the Universe.

The Divine Plan of
Eternal Spring for Earth,
the Truth of Life, Light,
and Love Divine and the reality
of one of your truths is...
you are the Bridge between Angels and Elementals
in the activity of *freely* co-creating
Limitless Physical Perfection upon my surface.
It is also worth considering
that when you listen or see the reports
of "news" of disruption,
that you, in your own unique way,
demand the Truth to re-qualify
the mis-qualified business of old world,
ego-driven, reporting.

You have come to my planet to:
a) Master Energy, Vibration, and Consciousness and
b) to create and repair. To heal altered perfection.
Just like Jesus commanded
of those who wished to follow him:
"Greater things shall ye do…"

My chosen destiny is to experience,
with my faculties as a Master,
perfection in form – here and elsewhere.

87°

Light Bearers,
oftentimes it is good to recall
the activity of flawless Illumination.
Remembering that we take action
in service to the whole planet and all people.
So, with sincere intent to Illuminate your Being,
first be still…
then visualize a White, Gold Flame or Sun
in the heart area for several breaths.
While holding that picture,
breathe up into your nostrils the Fiery Light.
Then on the out-breath,
see it instantly flash and fill the veins of the Earth.
So, it is to fill and to see you become
an ever brighter Golden Sun's Presence
and the Earth a White, Gold Sun of Freedom.

I dwell in pure Flame…
I breathe only Sacred Fire.

What I see and Feel for myself
I accept for the whole planet.

I Am the Light of the World
and all of the World is Light.

88°

Continuing, dear Co-Servers,
with what Love can do for you...
Give a moment of thought to
the Cosmic Threefold Flame in your heart.
It is a miraculous ditto of the Godhead
and it is all Power, Intelligence,
and Love Magnetism
that brings into tangible reality **anything,**
with all of the Celestial hosts
able to gather around it,
just like a Sun or Star...

Let's harness our superpower.
*Through the Presences
of God-being within my heart,
I pause and feel...*

*I ask that the greatest Powers
of the Greatest Healing Love
in all the Galaxies,
all the Cosmic Beings of Cosmic Love
who govern the Powers of Nature
and the Forces of the Elements,
unleash your Sacred Fire Power
through my call.*

Perhaps the greatest single knowing
an aspirant may have
is of the Threefold Flame
and Its God Radiation.
The light of God contains
all the *energy, matter, and intelligence*
needed to complete the Divine Plan
for all things.
Thus within this Light
is the Divine physical life force
that the Threefold Flame
is destined to govern in love.
As you see,
within *the Light* is both
the force of Divine Consciousness
and the force of Divine Potential
which, when *married in Harmony,*
gives birth to Limitless Physical Perfection.
The Threefold Flame is meant to govern
the physical realm.
It is not static
but blazes with active God qualities
that affect all functions
of body, mind, and spirit.
Just like a radiator anywhere in a room,
you see, Cosmic Holy Spirit literally radiates
through and out of this Threefold Flame
given to you to use.
If given **your attention,**
It **WILL** automatically supply all the experiences
that constitute Heaven on Earth:
peace, abundance, clarity, creativity, and so on.
Surrender to the **perfect flow**
already happening through your Cells (Temples).
In this, you find the perfection of every activity,
the Perfection of Being.

89°

Solar Friends of Earth's Freedom,
as we move ever deeper into our Solar being,
the awareness and use of the Sacred Breath
becomes ever more important.

Today may be a perfect day
to practice the Power of Conscious Breathing.
Choose, if you will, a breathing statement,
said silently, that will benefit all of life.

The Angels are the very Breath of God.

90°

To the many of us (you)
who upon my bulk
are wishing for the
immediate transformation
of the species,
I wish for you to remember
the Divine Plan of you
being the Bridge to Freedom that you are.

The scene on my planet
has gone so far into separation
that only the Greatest Powers in all of Creation
could possibly bring us all home safely.
Within this Power that You are
is the daily recognition
of the vast Celestial Force,
i.e. the 12 Great Elohim,
the finger and infinite Circle of the Godhead,
and all the Ascended Masters
who have gone before us.
Girded with these identities
you may become
the greatest healing and Freedom
to the Powers of Nature
and the Beings of the Elements.
If any of you were to call forth
the Sacred Fire Freedom
of all the powers of Heaven
to go before you in an infinite circle
and set all of Nature free from discord,
you would have instant feedback.
They will demonstrate their Love to you.
I Am a voice of Gaia.

91°

In the realm of Love's perfect Presence,
as we continue to actualize
the Great Divine Plan
for Earth and all Galactic life,
be not startled at the enormity of who you are,
present.
The great cosmic climax
is unfolding right here.
Rather, be busy about who you are.
On that note, the great virtue of Patience
(which is truly a phenomenon reserved
for worlds of form with emotional bodies)
and its sister, **Understanding,**
are the Key to being
the Harmony of your true Being.
It is the Key to the constant flow of your I AM.
You see, beloveds,
the presence of the greatest Love
of the Mother God Itself
is returning to my surface to be experienced/felt
by everyone who has chosen to stay on board.
This is why the Emotional Body
and the Etheric Body (memories)
must and are being renewed and brought Home.
Apply this if you feel:

As Captain of my World
and for all other life,
I intend to embody the fountain
and reservoir of Mother/Father God's
Cosmic Love to the Earth.
I Am one with this Way;
and this Way is filled with Cosmic Virtue,
with which I desire to bless the World.

92°

Fellow bringers of the New Light,
let's remember some keynotes:
I Am is God in action,
I Am everywhere present.
I Am the only authority.
I Am here to give,
even though giving and receiving
are the same thing.
I Am a Divine Director of Sacred Fire
and I Am Sacred Fire,
the whole activity of God.
The English word "God"
came from the word Good,
as in, "It's all Good."
Remember, our truest, True personal desire
is for all Humanity and for the totality of Earth
and her lifeforce to make the Ascension in this life
as gently as possible.
In the Now,
it is good to practice living the New Earth, literally.

You have stepped into the New Light
and the Beings of the Elements
are already doing as much as they can
to demonstrate this New Reality.

Just say Yes to Life…
It's that Yes! that will propel and assure everything.
Because, it is gratitude.

I Am an ambassador of Love.
I Am the Light of the World
and I Bless this Planet now.
Oh, Yes I Am, Yes I AM, the One.

93°

From the land of sky blue waters
and galactic green meadows,
we gather for the Ascension
of the rest of Humanity
that might dwell otherwise.
As stewards we naturally
keep our attention on the ball (of Light).
So, we may wish to realize
the highest science of wave into particle
through the activity of creation
with regards to the "children"
that are now on the planet.
They (or we) are of what could only be termed
"the Rainbow Infusion."
We are here to manifest at blow back speed
the hidden and the known structures of Grace;
Harmony's outrageous Authority
of infinite, boundless splendor,
the science of Crystalline Programming
or flow of Fragrance,
(Fragrance being like Sacred Fire).
We have proof of our accomplishments "on record."
We wish to just "do,"
like God-Beings in a supervised,
but unlimited, playground.
Till then, just hold a vision of Freedom.

***I Am the being of Light,
and I intend to see only Light acting here.***

94°

Friends of the Light,
who have put off your personal Ascension
until all who wish to enjoy the New Earth
in her new Orbit of Love's Purity,
it is for us to remember this
at this time of moving apart
into the different realities.
You see, it is now, that those
who with most of their hearts and minds
wish to continue with IOU's and karmic debt
will, of free will, continue.
Remember, you/We are here to provide a platform
of magical, alchemical assured outcome
for anyone who of their own Free Will
wishes Peace and plenty for all,
to experience the New Earth
in her new Orbit.
This is the meaning of her title:
The Star of Spiritual Freedom.

***Now what is paramount for us
is to have an identity
that is the Truth of our Being
and that is
a Sun of the Sun.***
As that identity you must know
that you are a global Sun of many Suns.
In this way you are seen from star ships,
in a big way. Yes?

95°

Masters, dear friends,
in response to the numbers of those
who are susceptible to the feeling
of discouragement and other fears,
we wish to remind you that you are here
as (and in) a very large group,
and because of recent great Dispensations
you are more seen and known even individually
than the condition of the whole group.
Please wrap your clear head around that
and feel its truth.

Secondly, as you know, you raised
your own hand (of God) to come here.
With joy and thrill you jumped into this
unprecedented plan of Love's Idea.

Thirdly, from this moment forth
your life is forever.
So, as we all move forward
from this delicious place we are at in the play
we are assured the highest outcome.
Just by remaining steadfast in the Realm of Cause,
and knowing the effects will all be "perfect."
Plus, beloveds,
the New Earth
and New Humanity
are already here,
as is the old.
Joy unspeakable, indeed.

Remember: ***I AM the Presence
and I am Its intelligent activity.***

96°

Friends of the Universe,
you who are the Song of the Suns,
considering that the Divine Plan
to return Earth folk
back to and caught up with
the already Ascended Universe,
you may realize the Great Commands
given by former Avatars...
such as, "Nothing matters for humans
more than knowing the God, I AM is them,"
and "Nothing is more important
than the raising of Humanity's Consciousness."
The application of these two fiats
would bring to the close the raising
of any of our animals for slaughter.

*The complete manifestation
of a new expression of the Universe
on Earth is **"the New Children"**
(some who are adult at this time).*

Also equal is staying humble
in the Revelation that
"What is about to transpire
is unimaginable in its magnitude."
I Am, a voice of Gaia.

97°

From out of the Great Silence
has come the Goddess of Peace,
to share Her Heart's Love with us.

"Constant lovers of Life in all Its forms,
it is that Constant Loving Kindness
which has no doubt or fear
that is my 'loudest' Song.
As the great Star Nations watch,
and the Earth is held in bated breath
during the pause of Grace,
the great Whales and Dolphins
finish their final touches
of 'packing it up'
for their long awaited return.
The other Tribal Indian
'Native' folks (nations)
also exhale the tone of finishing
and are off to their real Homes.
'Indian' means 'of God' (of Dios).
People of God.

"For you see most of the
'Indigenous, Aboriginal' nations stepped in –
came to this planet – to hold space,
to hold the Cause in certain lands where, or so,
the Light of Cosmic Love could create patterns
with the Elementals and other must haves.
In short, they (Cetaceans and most aboriginals)
are large groups from other systems,
who responded to the Call of Love
and service to the Whole.
We bid them adieu.

"It is Peace Divine, the final step
that allows our next experience.
I Am that Peace
and Its out-breath of security.

"To all the Great Whales,
Dolphins, and Aboriginal peoples
who have assisted in this:
My gratitude forever!"

98°

Eternal Friends,
from within a pool of the Rose Pink Ray I sing.
Of all the Beings within interstellar space,
the one with the most Angels
(which means Atmosphere)
is the Great Elohim of Peace.
He, Lord Tranquility, and Her, Lady Pacifica,
are perhaps as available to you
as your next precious breath.
First know that all 12 of the
Elohim's Heart Flames
are literally within and around your head.

They can and will guard your mental faculties,
just by your acknowledgment and thought.
Look into and learn about this great tool of Self.

Anyway, the Elohim of Peace wish to show you,
right now, how locally tangible They are.
Make a call from your Heart,
from that still Self,
on behalf of all other life as well:

Elohim of Peace,
Fill me with your Peace.
Still me with your Peace.
Thrill me with your Peace.

The decree as follows
will Ascend anyone to the heights:

I Choose Peace.
I Choose Peace.
I Choose Peace.

99°

Oh You, that Love alone could give to this World,
considering the magnetic power
of the Rose Pink Ray, an Invocation might be:

Through the Power of Love which I Am
and the full Presence within my heart,
I invoke all aspects of my Divinity and my Being
to fill, flood, and charge
my ever-expanding environment
with all the Love of all the Light
of Cosmic assistance to this Earth today.
Oh great Host of many,
use my Presence and Its aura
to the fullest that the Law will allow
to Raise every aspect of life
that needs assistance in any way!
Reveal your Hand of Holy Spirit,
just because I have passed their way,
even to the full circling of this globe.
I mean business and I Am the authority
of this Love, right here and Now.
I thank you all, with constant gratitude.

***I Am a global Sun of Divine Love
and I Am Its Cosmic Power.***

100°
Suns of Service

Children of the Suns, with eternal gratitude
and its immortal Joy do I project.
Returning to the reason of Truth
and your unquestionable identity,
let yourself visualize...
See and feel your entire inner self
as a dazzling White Fire-Light for a long moment.
Then, see a globe sun of Yellow Gold.
Become its expression.
Be sure to feel its Rays
go out from you in all directions...
Then, tune into a flow from above
and from beneath your presence.
Be still with this knowing for a while.
Now, as a master of service to the Highest,
intend and see and feel this (your Sun identity)
to flow directly out your feet
into the core of Love at the center of this Planet.
Now from your heart, qualify this flow
to be the blessing to any part of life
that you feel the most for at this moment.

Consider this:

***I Am a constant Cosmic pipeline
of the Greatest Light
and its laser of Love to the Center
of this blessed Planet.***

101°
Manifesting

Expanding from the Truth of stillness
and all the Peace it brings to You
in the use of Conscious Imaging,
one might ask,
"What of the power of visualizing?"
It is the unfailing real-time activity
of being God here.
The first thing one must know is that
the power to visualize (create a mental picture)
is the God Power acting, period.

Next is to know that it takes determined Will
(which doesn't happen much with humanity),
and right Now is the on-stage time
for that gathered Will to act.

Third, determine not to speak about
what you are visualizing to anyone,
and realize that the Host of Heaven's Guides
are assisting you to find and sequester time
to ***practice*** *this creative act that never fails,*
if given enough of your Gift of Life's Energy.

I Am a Voice of New Earth and I speak your Truth.
You can have anything you want or see.

102°

Friends of Truth,
Life may wish us to continue our Power thought.
Just be with the Action beating your heart.
First choose a cause you wish to be a part of.
Affirm that the Light has all the matter
and intelligence required here.
Acknowledge the vast Forces of Life
attending your cause.

*As a Divine Director
of Life on this planet
I now invoke
the Greatest Cosmic Light of Source
into the center of this sweet Earth,
through me.
I see the Earth, a White Sun
with Oceans of Violet Fire.
I see the marriage of the two.
Center and surface become
a perfect Lilac, Lavender Fire Light
of Purity's Freedom.*

*I decree that this Vision of my Self
is one with the vast Group
of Ascended Humanity.
Sustained, free of any limit,
I Am the Gathering of Truth
and I Am Its Freedom here.*

103°

Dear cells of the body of Universal I Am on Earth,
as we continue unabated in assimilating
all other cells whose attention still goes
to fear or greed,
it is the Harmony of your Total True Being
and Its Seat of Power
that is the *acting* Presence
that, in time, does for those
what they may otherwise be too far
from doing for themselves.

***For the present purpose is
to anchor the Consciousness
of True Being and the Supremacy of Love***
into enough of the neighborhoods to prevail.
This is why we "need" you empty of self
and Breathing as *One with the Way.*

This is impersonal in the extreme
as the ***Purpose now is for the whole.***
So, as a science, we must hold to the service
of what are known as Harmonizer Cells,
Who sing a new purpose at hand,
Constantly…

104°

Great Host of Love's return to Earth
and her governance.
It is I, Micah, and in the full union
of Heaven and Earth's Consciousness
do I transmit this day.
As you know,
all life is innocent from the beginning.
So that makes the ease and Truth of Unity a win
in any court of Justice to and for all life.
One example of this will be the swift return
of those who have chosen to remain on New Earth
and return to the accurate treatment
of our animal folk.
Just like "No more poverty consciousness,"
so, no more "I need animal protein, blah, blah."
In Unity Consciousness,
one face looks at the other face
and has already chosen an act
to raise that one into greater
more expanded expression.
Just like our beloved Earth/Gaia
has done for us Now.

Life, as it is, is awesome.
I Am.

105°

Gentle Co-Servers of the raising
of Humanity's Consciousness,
it is a perfect moment to remind myself
that this Great Mission of Light
to Earth and her Souls
is One of demonstrating the use of
Energy, Vibration, and Consciousness.
The first act is to Remember
it is my "job" to live and enjoy the Reality
of what the Great Mighty Elohim
and Cosmic Beings
(Jesus, Mary, Saint Germain, etc.)
have put in place–the tangible,
walk-able, plant-able New Earth.
I Remember the program.
We will create the new planet,
but it will–for a while–only be
accessible by consciously choosing!
Remember, Children of the Sun,
this is an act of Mercy and allowing.
Remember the mission is
a highly advanced *act of Consciousness*.
Contemplate this, my beloved self.

I Am here to give–and it is already here.

106°

Lovers of Peace, we love to be where Love is.
You know, expectancy is a wonderful Tool
for the student to use,
because it both self-teaches one
all the fundamentals of the Law
and the absolute momentum of expectation
always, always shows results/manifestation.
Push through and clear away
any other chatter and choose,
for instance, Eternal Youthfulness.
You just create your own unique
rhythm of joyful expectancy
(decrees, smiling, breath-work, etc.)
and nothing else will manifest for you.

*At any moment any of us **will shift** into
the indestructible Solar, Light Substance that is
the next Now expression of the Human species.*
FOR ALL OTHER LIFE,
expect the New Earth to manifest
for those ones too.
Have great expectancy for
**Divine Love's Power to do for
and transform others.**
And Transform those ones.
I Am a voice of Gaia,
and I Am the Angel Deva of Expectation,
for You!

107°

Dear Servers to others,
this moment with you shall be given to
"As I am raised up
so shall all life be raised up with me."

The directive "Take time to be Holy"
is of paramount importance
at this busy Cosmic Moment.
You see, all that must come to the surface –
literally on my surface (daily life) –
shall come out to be loved free.
Hence, because it is the Light in action
bringing the "stuff" up, we must all **be** the Light.
We BE the Light by Feeling the Love of Source;
by *"Be still and know That I Am."*

Also the Great Armadas of Galactic Star Neighbors
and Inner Earth relations
are about to move into a next step
of the *cohesive plan.*
The Plan is that we **demonstrate**
the Harmony of our True Being
as unwaveringly as possible.

All things are "possible"
when we are the Light
and only the Light of the Core of Love.
I Am.

108°
An Invocation

Oh Great and Total Self, all that I Am,
Raise my outer self this day
and come forth through this outer self today,
that there be no form of separation.

As me, right here and now,
pour through the greatest Light
of the greatest Love from the Heart of Creation
to all life that my aura can possibly contact.
See to it that all life around me
is raised into greater Perfection,
just because I have passed its way.
So it is and I Am grateful.

109°
Way Out

Remember Union?
Do you remember boarding
scintillating, live, crystalline starships
heading out to specific galactic ports of call?
You may recall gazing out a window,
upon the multi-billion twinkles
of friendly evolutions
whose trillions of assorted Beings share experience.

Earth is in deep outer space.
In fact, quadrants set for arrival
to this Solar System
are considered "way out there."
Let alone attempting to **"get"**
to 3D human events (time).

Regarding the Real Now...
"Decree a thing and so shall it be for you."

I Am a vast multidimensional Being
of great Light.
I Am the open, pure Heart
through which flows
The Age of Freedom to all Humanity.
That I Am.

110°
Some New Kids

Beloveds, I bring You a word
from the Middle Earth Children:

We broadcast our thrill and happy exuberance,
of what is now our imminent "Coming Out Event."
Even though so many surface people
have not yet stood up shoulder to shoulder
and used the Force of the Will of Love
to override the "foul balls,"
we have the power of You and your Calls
and Desires (Will) for Re-Union.
Do You "get it?" The New Earth,
the New Human, the Super Plan is flawless.
The greatest manifesters in all the Heavens
have been and are being born as "children"
by natural Law.

*We simply step in and bring the Chi Fun
and the Get-out-of-our-way Forcefield
through our majority numbers.
Anyway, we are on our way and we are ecstatic.
Make way and "tally ho!"*

We are the real "new kids on the block"
and we are untouchable, so to speak.

111°
The Expanded Mind

You, the individual of the global group victory,
the presence of the one great Presence,
Universal I Am.
What wondrous creation are You, the I Am,
going to give your life energies unto today?
We remember Who You Are.
To add to your Joy,
it will be useful to keep close
the greater Truth of this moment, which is:
What is underway is the Ascension focus
of the whole Human race,
as compared to the focus of our previous lifetimes,
which was Individual Ascension.
It is Wise to stay close to this activity
of Love for all underway.
One reason is that You will stay onboard
with the greater flow.
If your Heart leads you to prosperity and
abundance, consider using the expanded Mind.

Contemplate this:

"What pictures am I holding?"

Practice bright vibrant Visualization.

112°

From within the curves and the folds
of the soft Pink Flame
and its infinite flexibility of Divine Love
I project:

This is the end of a long journey
with the tyrannical aspect
of the lower human ego
at the illusionary throne of daily life.
Some of the good people of Earth,
as you know,
still will be counting on
a "Jealous God," "The Only Way,"
and the systems that are based on
fear and greed.

So, you, as the master of your destinations,
have chosen with clear intent to Ascend
from this moment forward.
It is Grace that will allow these systems
to collapse around you.
This Grace will have within it the structure
to stay on track with the upward rushing force.

True Freedom is Group Compassion.
Your Causal Body is the Key.

113°

Beloved friends,
victorious, upright, unshakeable,
Lovers of True Power.
The "brass tacks" of what we are all a part of is this:
This sweet little Planet is the meeting ground
for what has been, and is now to be,
the Cosmic Climax of all previous showdowns
in any Galaxy, in any System
heretofore ever played out.
Hence the "big cats" from both sides of the fence
are all present. This means **you.**

Be aware and understand that the "foul ball" aspects
of our One family have provided the most wicked
weaponry that is meant to baffle and surprise us,
even the very "Elect,"
into bowing and giving them your attention,
more than just your observing attention.

The Freedom "side of the fence" is **us.**
We are here to keep doing the daily task
of constant loving kindness and Harmony
at all turns.

Remember the movie "Avatar" when
all the forest animals showed up – BINGO!

114°

Dear Co-Servers, as the Beings of the Elements
have taught us, by demonstration:
See clearly the thing that you wish for
or see the perfect outcome
of what you desire to construct.
You may see any body of water that is polluted
as clear and blue.
Just see it with your *Joy of service,*
and it will manifest.
This is the missing *activity*
of many of those who are concerned.

The bulk of the planet moves forward
at geometric speed into Her
set of prescribed adjustments
before She bursts into the White Star
of Spiritual Freedom,
which every rock and drop of water strongly desires.
The desires mentioned here
are the Love of our Feeling Body.
Take time to be Holy
and to see with Crystal Vision.

115°

Co-Servers of the one Power,
I Am a Voice of True Being,
Humanity's Truth.
A reminder: You and I are here to assist the
"Forced Raising of Human Consciousness."
Much like children still in the pool,
after Mom and Dad have asked them many times
to get out and load up into the vehicle.
Contemplate this!

We are here to use our creative faculties,
our Thoughts and Feelings, with the Power of
"*I AM* the one thinking these thoughts." Period.

How shall you or anyone remain
in the steadfast Peace and Harmony
of your True Being as chaos runs its course?
We have shown ourselves
by what Jesus and others have done
by standing (in their Truth) on the shore
and commanding the storm to cease,
or feeding hundreds with the crumbs on hand.
Best said: Who you are is not ***Who you are.***
Who You are is the I AM.

A burst of *Group Compassion*
would instantly change everything
of Nature's Form called, daily life.
I Am the Spirit of Truth.

116°

Dear Friends and neighbors,
during this moment of metamorphosis
that we are all in,
this Ascended Masters' teaching
may be of unsurpassed assistance
for those who wish to give
on a cosmically free level
to the animal and Nature realms around you.

This, we share, is about being in conscious,
coherent, cogeneration with Sun Gods
and great Solar Beings.
First contemplate:
Be with all of the matrix
of Sacred Fire that you are
(Heart Flame, Head Flame, Chakras, etc.).
Then see and know the Light Rays projecting
to whatever part of Life you wish to assist.
Simultaneously realize the re-animation
of the Flame–of the Sun that you are–
and take command of that piece of Life.
This is the Way and the Nature of Sacred Fire
expanding the Universe.

I Am a Being of Flame and
I Am Its Light re-creating life on Earth.

117°

As we each know so well,
the sinister ones will do all they can
to get, hold, and keep our attention.
Which, by the way, says a lot
about who you truly are – about your Truth.
In order to command a balanced life style
(and through you others will get this)
one thing the great Host of Many taught us
back when the "world was coming to an end"
during a previous shift upward was:
This day, I qualify every thought
of my Mind to be Perfection.
I demand every feeling out from me
to be Perfection because I Am Perfection
and I Am creating.
Now, if you have a rough time
feeling your God Self acting,
simply close your eyes
and see only Light Substance.
And, if you wish, call upon
any Masterful Presence of your liking
to assist and be with you in your Vision.
Remind yourself again and again
to ask yourself the question
What pictures am I holding?
This has never been more meaningful
in any life you have ever lived.

I Am a Powerful Quantum Forcefield
raising all life within and around me.

I Am the Presence
and I Am Its intelligent activity.

118°
Peace Commander

Beloveds of the New Children
of absolute Freedom,
You are our oneness.
As the Age of God
steadily assimilates everything
unto Its next expression, we breathe
easily, deeply, and rhythmically.
In truth, just the invocation,
"I Am breathing easily, deeply, and rhythmically,"
as you silently hold that Perfect Picture
of your desire for that moment,
would be a wonderful exercise in "Mastery."

To quell any confusion about the disregard
and insane disrespect for the Earth
and Her realms still ongoing;
remind yourself daily that
humanity's belief structures
are ancient and deep.
This moment is about
The Miracle Ascension of the Whole,
back to Love and Love alone.
Then we will be in swift and practical
rebuilding of the Eco-Systems with
All Life Reunified On Earth.
Any time you wish to use your power,
go out on your back lawn or anywhere
and, to the discord in the atmosphere say:

***I Am the Peace Commanding Presence
and I say, "Silence."***

119°
Our True Identity

Life wishes you, the individual, to know that We are and
there is the embodied force-field of Divine Love
so powerful right now that no gathering
of ego desires can thwart
our mission.

Now the Way to
assure Its and Our graceful
flow is to identify yourself as the
Highest aspect of God, Source, or Life and
really *See and Know That*. See your Heart Flame
from beneath your feet to above the top of
your head and out from around you.
Or see your very Presence as
a Sun of great Light,
of great Love.

The important thing is to Identify your Self.
Who You are is Love Supreme in action.

I Am a Sun of Love.

120°
A Divine Director

Beloved Friends of True Being,
I greet you in the feeling of the crimson
Ruby Red Flame of Ministering Grace.

Most all of us are afraid of our Power.
I wish to speak into your Divinity.
Who you are is That I Am.
Who you are is God,
the great creative Heart of Universal I AM.

I remember harnessing Universal I AM
through dedicated choice
and the constancy of my attention.
Instantaneous healings ensued.
The "dead" were reanimated.
I bring this memory up now because
there is nothing that has been hidden
that shall not be revealed.

We spoke previously of our Power
to direct the Elements
and watch, as they do our bidding.
Let's think upon this *structure of Grace.*

It is the Power of Identity.
In **absolute Oneness.**
Unto, *being a director of the elements.*

121°
Alpha and Omega

An Invocation:

Oh beloved I Am, my total God Self, I love You.
Come forth. Fill, flood, and charge
this our outer self and world,
that I am privileged to qualify.

Great Self, I call You forth!
Come forth and project our Sun-like Qualities
out of every faculty of my body here on Earth.
Come through my eyes as Mother's Love Light.
Come through my voice as Father's loving Authority.
Project out of my ears as a regional scanning
of limitless Hearing, through my pores
as a comforting Sacred Fragrance.

Today I take my outer self in hand
and my one demand is that all of it
be the Out-breath of Cosmic Love.
See to it that all I contact this day
are raised into greater Perfection,
just by my passing their way.

I Am the Mother/Father
Sun/God loving life free.

I Am the Magic Presence.

122°

I Am the Collective of Mount Shasta.
I, like you, am the Heart of this World.
Though I, being of the Volcanic expression,
am also the Mind of this Mission.
Volcanoes are "a piece of my Mind," so to speak.
As the Essence of Holy Spirit, Mother God/
Cosmic Love "takes over," be aware of,
or think about, great Grand Triangles.
Always in the act of creating Permanence,
from Source do we use the Triangle.
It is the first manifest thoughtform
of Elemental Perfection around a Heart Flame.

We have shared a few triangulations
that our Love Forces to the Earth have wished
the awakening ones here to energize.
This Mission is vast and has many aspects
and areas of life participating.
It could be visualized and felt that
Mount Shasta is the Heart of the Crown Chakra,
that Brazil is the base/bottom of the Heart,
and that France is the dance of the Flames.
Or, whatever comes to Mind for you, beloved.
Also, for the Light that must come
through the North Americas,
see the great Rays of Light from Me,
over to the east, to Montreal,
then down, over to the Royal/Grand Tetons.

Though you are the Master,
so whatever you choose to energize is perfect.

***I Am the Forcefield of Love's Victory,
causing Humanity to Remember.***

123°

Beloved Lighthouses of my being,
I am Earth, Gaia.
Now that you have determined
to know that you are a Sun–God in constancy–
I wish to express my Gratitude,
that it may finish a Circle of Gratitude.

Well, my Friends, as Suns on my surface
you are the Animating Principle,
the actual vibrancy that is visible
to all that look at me.

Our oneness is just that–One.
Our love affair takes on a new octave
of Dancing for the many.
Recall how you first saw some couple dancing...
You were *MOVED* and desired to experience
that for yourself. Yes?

This is what we, or shall I say,
the Divine Plan, in Its exactness, is.
We teach by demonstration.

What is important is that we be not
broken into or apart by any appearance
of imbalance (foul music).
Ask for Illumination
and then breathe It up–
from your Heart Flame.
Right into your Head.

124°

Oh useful Suns of the Great Central Suns
that you are, at this rarest of moments
and as the whole Celestial Neighborhood looks
with bated breath at their crystal screens
toward the next moment and step of the birth...
Be it a reminder that the first fruit
of our Cosmic Consciousness is
constant loving kindness.
Also, "seek Wisdom, but get Understanding."

Remember this:

***I AM raising the Consciousness
of an entire planet.
This is my reason for being.***

What really matters?
Well, perhaps it is how much Cosmic Light
of the Great New Rays, that Law requires
the god Beings on the planet
to "wish" for, which can flow
to, through, and out from us,
unabated.
This is only accomplished
by moment-to-moment Harmony.
Much is riding on our gentle Power of
Total True Being.

125°

Reflecting, as Suns do,
back on our gathered Truth,
it is good to remember that we are a
committed member of the biggest action
of the greatest Minds of Love's Power
ever implemented unto the untangling
and saving of an ensnared World.

Your Immortal, Victorious Heart Center
is just that – Immortal and Victorious.
Now, to "remember" is to
become a member once again
of your Knowingness.
Even many times a day if it be appropriate.

Ahh, indwelling Presence come forth.
Take command of this moment and onward.
Just re-establish this outer self
and all of our faculties as a fountain
and reservoir of my total I Am Self.
Surround me with all activities
of the Sacred Fire
and see to it that all I contact
are raised and assisted.

To all the Ancestors and Inner Guides helping,
I Am so grateful.

126°

Special Forces of Love Supreme,
We ask this of each other and we,
of necessity, must contemplate this...

Many of us know that we are here as a group
and that **"greater things shall ye do."**
It takes a "small group of devotees"
to effect the whole of Nature.
Please consider stepping into a
"Daily Group Assistance"
to all of Nature and Humanity.
This includes those who are on a
destructive path (for now) as well.
So they can move on ASAP.

So now we re-up this receivership
by stepping-up and harnessing our Superpower.
Feel this Truth.
When a majority of Humanity
releases a burst of *Compassionate Feeling*
of healing intent to life, on Earth,
The Whole of Daily Life Will Change, Instantly.
We create the "starter."
We leave this to your Mastery to contemplate.

Next, we will choose and choose again
as a "large group" of Universal I AM,
doing on Earth.

I Am the One making this Call
in the One, for the One, and as the One.
I Am the Mother/Father God
preparing the next enormous leap.

127°

Eternal Friends,
please re-read the previous memo.
We, that is, the One I Am acting,
has asked that we accept
that Now is the time
we gather and nurture
this Feeling of Compassionate Kinship
with every part of life,
humanity and nature.
To know that we will magically send it out
in a next moment.
In a burst of Power
so much will instantly change
(like a "dead" one called out of a tomb).
In *that,* we will have caught up with
the hopes and prophesies of all the former
great ones who spoke about this exact moment.

Here is what I suggest:
Today keep breathing into and feeling
the *back of the heart* where this
"E-Motion" will register.
Feel and Know that we are preparing to experience
a group outburst of Compassion that will
Heal and Transfigure "everything," *Instantly.*
I send it out, myself now.

Do you realize the uncountable
Celestial and Inner Earth attendance
that will be on-board with this?

***I AM the One
and We mean business here.***

128°

Dear voices of Heaven's sake,
we are the Host of many.
It is with great heart that we ask of you,
who do so much already,
to consider creating, then amplifying
and empowering an Avatar-like
(in your very own unique way),
God Feeling of Superpower,
and release it into the atmosphere.
This is something that is intended Consciously,
though organized and managed entirely
by the Inner Self.
This is a Prayer, being called forth from the Inner
of those who are slipping downward
under the weight.
We are here to raise Humanity's Consciousness
and to Heal life.
This is an act of Conscious healing power
of the greatest ever hoped for.
As Jesus did, drop the agendas
and answer the call to
"heal the sick and raise the dead."

Consider this:

Regarding the need of the hour,
I Am here and I Am there.
So, I "magically" show-up and re-create everywhere.

We are the Power of Love being called for.

129°

So how does it feel, having a career
in the Light, as the Light?...
as the return of the I AM Presence in residence...
as literally being the energies that flow
along our Meridians of Light.
This is the long-awaited moment
for our manifest intent to be
the full embodiment of our Total Universal Being
and re-take command (from the little ego)
and create the daily lives of Limitless Physical
Perfection and Its Justice for all other life here.

What fun...to contemplate the act...
knowing we are, or knowing
I Am here as a group.

"Here is I AM"
is a wonderful statement.
Regarding the fun I mentioned:
We know that experiences of great sorrow
("the wailing and gnashing of teeth")
will be a part of our relations'
(Humanity's) Transformation.
We acknowledge the long-standing stance
of refusing Change, referring to that momentum
that is in our cells and nervous system.

And so it is, we have a career in the Light –
the Ascended Masters born and raised on Earth.
In the World. Loving life free.

130°

Dear Lovers of Life,
I ask that we harness our power and make this call
on behalf of our assured, immediate future.
Some are aware that you are designed to look for
and harness the great Cosmic Rays
that Home is directing to Earth.
Now is one of those auspicious moments.
If you are so promoted, you will certainly feel
the many who Stand and work with you.

Beloveds, our younger ones are the fullness
of the New Age and its Structure of Grace
that this Earth and daily life are about to experience
(with or without me)
the great Crystalline Technologies of freedom's flow,
the building powers and abilities
(that the new children have in their resumés)
that most would not believe
lest you saw it with your own eyes.
These new ones are the Master Builders of Grace
and Perfection's Joy.
We should make a call together to assist in their
Protection to assure their Freedom to manifest.

First be in perfect stillness.
***Oh great Life, That I AM, which I Am,
and Great Host of Protectors of the New Life,
the young ones.
I demand the greatest Powers of Light
enfold and seal the whole Lifestream
of each of our precious young ones
and my Heart's Love and Blessing go to them,
without limit, constantly.
I thank You.***

131°

Dear Servers of others,
within the realm of service to Worlds gone wild,
it is Hoped that we, "The Away Team,"
will not only take quiet time to be Holy,
but also ask the questions often:

How today will I be the Heart,
Head, and Hands of God here?

How might I bring forth greater expressions
of Harmony and Peace
and demonstrate the supremacy
of Spiritual Freedom on Earth?

How could I show the Joy and Thrill of God being,
through acts of Breathing, Posture,
Dance, or Smiling?

What on Earth am I going to do today
to glorify Life and raise all that I contact?

Almighty Presence within,
reveal to me the Perfect things to do,
and through me, as me, do it all, so perfectly.
I Am grateful.

132°

Radiant Beings of Love ablaze,
we greet and commune with one another
from the Heart of the Mission.
During this moment together, let's acknowledge
Power and Its First Cause for all Life:
Perfection, for all things.
Consider, if you will,
the Power aspects of the Center Point of Love
(this is a Love-based Universe).
One would be Protection.
Another may be the "Demand" of Love.
The word and use of the word "Demand"
will raise questions and furrow brows
in the western world of Earth's school.
We are referring here to the vast East and West,
to the complex denial of Humanity's Power
and Its Freedom from the beginning,
and It's desire to be expressed Freely.
And to do so without concern for anyone's opinion.
Period.

Next is the dance of knowing who you are
and staying attached only to Love.

We know this is a big subject matter
and we know, also, of your Pure, God-Free Power.
Use these statements:

***I Am the Rod of God,
and I gather the Circle of stability.***

***I Am here and I Am there,
and I Am the only Presence acting there.***

133°

Friends of the Light and doers of Love,
I love your Presence.
I am thoughtful of your individual person
and what you truly desire.
I stand with tears running down my face,
with all we have been experiencing so far
and all that is yet to come.
It is said,
"You teach best what you need to know the most."

My Mission mates,
this is the moment of bated breath.
It is going to take a lot of Love –
the Cosmic Love of the initiate –
to fulfill the Divine Plan
and to assure the minimum intervention
for the real Great Divine Plan
to be a whopping success.
It is and will require,
a significant quotient of the awakened,
being the *infinite flexibility of Divine Love*,
to magically assist those who are still carrying
the wearisome weight of returning energies.
The "Magic" will absolutely transform
those around us during the "gripping" moments
of our Planet's re-emergence.

"Cosmic Love" is a powerful term
to use and to contemplate.
Yours.

134°
Divine Tenacity

You who are available for service to the Whole
here on the surface,
you may remember that within the Forcefield
of Divine Love reclaiming this World,
the activity of Purity is one of
the first deliberate choices.
Then Resurrection, then Ascension –
all being one White Ray and its flow.
We mention this because
the Great First Cause, the Blue Intent Ray,
is most active towards Earth at this time.
The marriage or combination
of these two Flames and Rays
is the atomic core of the "Immaculate Concept."
It is best utilized through us
as determination and tenacity
toward that which you wish to add to or be,
as the next Ray and Quality.
For instance, see the whole of your Inner Bodies
as a dazzling White with some hue of Blue,
then choose a Color to emanate
as your invitation at this time.
You will instantly feel
the Power behind this Cosmic Love.

***I Am the Immaculate Concept
of Humanity's Freedom on Earth.***

135°
Giving Back
To Nature

Dear Presences, We and I wish to speak
of that which only Love can give.
You who love and hope for Nature and the Elements,
I join with you in bringing to them
the most powerful assistance Life can give them.
We can bring and hold a balance to prevent
the destructive use of their Gifts and Blessings
that are still being wrongly used.
Call forth the Love of your own I Am
and call to the Great Host who govern
the Powers of Nature and Forces of the Elements
and ask that this Love and Its Power
go to, dissolve, and consume
any and all impurity whatsoever,
everywhere, and add,
"I ask that this Call be amplified seven billion times,
as I am 'The One' with all Humanity."

I assure you, the Beings of the Elements
will further gather around to
protect, supply, and bring Blessings
to you and to your World.
They are Intelligent and group oriented
more than you may know, dear friends.

136°

Radiators of Love's Victory,
I share with you from within the Mind of Life.
You may recall **the Way of Unity Consciousness,**
the way of, "You can't have one without the other."

If you are at a place where this makes sense to you,
you will appreciate the full use of one's
full attention upon and within The Mind.
(If you were to meet an advanced
fully open-Hearted Celestial Master of creation
who was "all up in Her head" with Her power,
you would be in awe and humbled
before Her great creative focus of Love's Mind.)

Many of us here know that
we are Elohim in training –
the highest graded order
of an Elemental Being.
Elementals use mental powers
to bring the outer form into being.
Now is the time to mentally focus
on any Central Sun of your choice
and concentrate on Its Magnet of Love.
"The Great Central Sun's Magnet of Love,"
which will magically create
Unity Consciousness en-mass.
Contemplate this.

What greater demo do we have of
"what I do surely affects the whole,"
than a Sun in the Heavens?

137°

Family of miracle Love,
Together Standing in the Light is our only stance.
We who have chosen Peace shall not be moved.
With these two Truths ablaze upon our breath,
we remember.

*"In the fullness of the Presence
is the Love that I require.
In the fullness of the Presence
are all the Things that I desire."*

Miracle Love, as our Group ID,
refers to the legend in the Universes
of what we truly are to this
seemingly ensnared planet and race.
Love and Love alone has seen to it
to Reclaim all into Her Jurisdiction.

As we set to experience
*the Miracle of **Unity Reality**,*
accepted and invoked by the local population,
realize that the Heavens (stars and constellations)
will ***be allowed to reveal
what has already happened.***
A bit of "white knuckled" and "just hold on"
will inevitably ensue.

Because it has already changed. Completely.

***I Am the entirely New Cosmic Reality revealed
with Holy Spirit softening the emotions.***

138°

Unifiers of that which has called for redress,
as we breathe deeper into the full Re-Unification
of all Life, on the surface of our planet,
know and feel that there is no such thing as death
anywhere in the Galaxies.
This knowing is an ingredient
vital to the Victory won.
Contemplate this.
As you know so well,
a different sort of workable daily life
is going to burst out
and it is simply not for everyone
to go through the metamorphosis
at this time,
though EVERYBODY "makes it."
Understand?

A Song for Now might be...
***I Am, I Am, I Am the Blessing
and I Am the Miracle.
Oh yes, I Am the Doer, I Am the Doing,
and I Am the Deed well done!***

***My Gratitude is my service forever, for-ever,
and I Am the One Singing this Song...***

139°

Family of Light,
It is a miracle to be walking the Earth.
Souls are lined up from here to Arcturus
to participate in and get the experiences
from the Quantum Leap, the dimensional shift,
on a planet that has gone this far and long
into separation with so many billion souls...
back to the rule of Love.
Part of the desire of the many
who wish to be here with us,
is the fact that in all of creation,
nowhere else has any planet
received so much help
by so many of the greatest forces of interstellar,
big behemoth Cosmic Beings of Light.
It is good and powerful for our evolution
to contemplate and express our loving *gratitude*,
back to this actuality.

It is a miracle to be walking the Earth,
and no matter what the appearance
of the outer world,
I Am so grateful to have been given
a privileged embodiment at this moment.
I Am so grateful.

140°

Neighbors of Love,
it is wonderful to be speaking together at this time,
for this is the hour when our "kitchens" bring forth
the new menu that we have all shopped for,
for so many "days."
This is really the place where your "I Am"
is folding all time and space,
meaning I Am the perfect health,
eternal youthfulness, and radiant beauty.
Oh yes I Am! IS *right now* and onward,
deliberately out-picturing...
So again, "What pictures are you holding?"

I tell you, dear friends,
regarding EVERYTHING that you wish for:
a new society, new education for the young,
new daily life, a new body of youth, flexibility...
the greatest Power here is the knowing
and use of the Sacred Fire of God,
which is the Presence beating your heart.
But also more than that.
The Sacred Fire is from a few powerful sources
you should look into and know of.

141°

Bringers of the New,
We love you, We thank you, We Bless you!
"We" being all of us
remembering that "I Am" everywhere.
Truly, thou art God.
And to Light only do I bow.
Wisdom?
The Wise One is the one who loves.

Returning to the chat,
regarding the one thing that will set you free –
completely Free – in the most efficient ways
to move through the collapse
and re-emerging of a New Earth…
First, know that the gift of
the Violet Flame of Freedom's love
is the reason that our Earth is still inhabitable.
Second, know that you are here to wield (project) It,
in any way that you possibly can,
to all other life out and around you.
Because "Thou art God."
You and I are the One that is here
on behalf of others who are
weighted down or otherwise caught.
The Out-breath of the Violet Flame is everything
that those who require assistance of any kind
could ever Hope for.
"We" thank you for your love.
The *Violet Fire is perhaps your best friend,*
at this time.

***I will use, use, and use
the Transmuting Power
of the Sacred Violet Fire.***

142°
Attention

Friends of the Truth,
from the inside of this privilege comes a jewel
so needed by most at this moment.
That is the return to the knowing
of how powerful your attention is.
Please be with this Truth sometime soon.
You know the fundamentals,
and you know of your Divinity.
Now the most helpful thing for you might be
the Understanding of the application of
the Power of your *Attention*. This could be
the much needed assistance to get you (us) through
the tumults and possible chaos that will surely come
as my Body, the Planet, moves into a correct axis
and other "less holy" things abound,
within the next moments/days from now.
(I am scheduled for this shift.
It is an appointment.)
For instance, if you were to put your Attention
on your God-Self first,
then the Sacred Fire Love
from Venus or the Sun, *to the Earth*...
becoming a focus
and an **outpouring to others** of That...
you would catapult yourself into
Ascended Master evolution.

Your daily Attention is the thing for this.

143°
Using Sacred Fire

Friends, some have asked,
"What is the way and how is it
that we can best get the benefits of
the Sacred Fires, and their Sacred Flames,
for total freedom from old energies?"
In the morning, begin by stilling the mind
and identifying yourself from a center
in the chest area
as a Gold Sun filling and pushing
into and out through everything.

Then see a flow of Purple or Lavender Flame
rise from your heart, up through your head
(neck and chin rolling upward).
As you do, notice the Violet Flame pillar
from beneath your feet rising up
all within and around you.

And/or see the Pink, Gold, and Blue
steadily rise from below,
all around you completely enfolding your Being.
From any one of these Realities,
ask your Guides or the Beings from the Sun,
from Venus, etc., to add Their Sacred Love
of Their Sacred Fire and keep it sustained.

I Am a Divine Director of Sacred Fire.
I Am Sacred Fire, the Whole activity of Life.

144°

So, what is one facet of the realm of 144,000
we might use to actualize the Solar Being
of Cosmic Love's Illumination?

The Sacred Twelve.
Perhaps the most applicable now
is the Thoughtform of the Twelve Suns
of the Central Sun(s)
that our galaxies are based upon,
as far as re-creation goes.
Understand that, because of Life
choosing experimentation as part of Its Way,
the reason for seven and nine Chakras/Suns
is in order to step down into
Worlds of "denser" form.
Now we are re-turning,
into a Twelve Ray Being, very quickly.
In fact, nowhere is there a precedent
on the books of such an event happening
to such a large population, anywhere!

Mother Mary speaks:
*"You, beloved, are gathering all 144,000 aspects
of yourself back into this moment of Now.
It is called the Hologram,
where every ongoing experience
or all parts of you that are Consciousness
are being assimilated into the
'God's outer world experience of now.'
It is all Love.
Nothing exists outside of Love..."*

Here is a listing of how
these chakras out-picture in colors.
They are "Embodied" from head to tail.

                crown – Yellow Gold
            third eye – Emerald Green
             medulla – Aqua
              throat – Blue
             thymus – Magenta
               heart – Pink
      bottom of heart – Deep Gold
upper solar plexus – Peach
lower solar plexus – Ruby
           stomach – Amethyst/Violet
             sacral – Opal
                base – Ascension White.

***I Am a Solar Being on a Solar Planet
living Solar Realities.
I Am Ascended and Free...
and on and on we go.***

p.s. You are not even "limited" to the above.

145°

Creator Flames of God walking the Earth,
I come to chat a moment with regards to
the reality of our homecoming
and our rebuilding of the new systems
that are "taking place."
I will speak of the air element.

Within the Way of creation that takes place
on all formed realms (physical worlds, etc.)
the element of Air is in direct correlation
to and with the mental body.
It is the first fruit one uses to establish form...
There has been a long-time agenda to deny people
fresh air by those who would "profit"
from having your mental powers thwarted.
This is coming to a climax.

It is air that allowed you – first –
to become an individualized presence.
You see, as a "human" in the womb
you were not yet allowed to participate in outer/
planned creation until your first breath.
In short, we are entering the "Age of Air."

Bear in mind that with the use
of the four elements,
three of them act as a (or form the) cup.
The other is the Leader and is always present.
This is why invoking Sacred Fire
is all that is really necessary
while holding the Harmony
and Blazing the Light.

146°

Unto You who wish to help
in the most efficient way possible,
let us remember:
It is the Sacred Fire's activity
that has the most multidimensional,
magical powers of Intelligence Supreme.
It is designed to pour through you here
and accomplish,
for all other life that you contact,
unimaginable assistance toward
their greater Freedom,
just because you passed their way.
You see, beloveds, it is that the Divine Plan
calls for the Ascension of the whole now,
during this great *Cosmic Moment
of Grand Cycles converging* here on Earth.
Contemplate this.

The simple acknowledgment
of the Fire beating your heart
and the Fires giving you mental capacity
replicating throughout your body's cells,
is your certain Victory.

Hence the Victory of the Group
and our Greater Divine Plan.

147°

As I Stand
in rapt awe facing the majesty of Life,
I notice myself exhaling
in tones that are birthed from that awe.
Having of recent felt the Rays
(of Cosmic Love) entering my field,
and now, seeing Its unfoldment, everywhere,
I ask – because I Am – Humanity to just Love.
Which means Heal and Love Free
every altered (old tape, old creation) human emotion
that is less than what is Real and Permanent
for a Sustainable Community.

What is preparing Itself
to envelop and restore to Humanity,
because It must be restored,
is a Love that has not been remembered
or known for many millions of our years
here on Earth.
The story is long in the what, where, and why's,
but there really is no time left
to dig in to "the story."

This Love is the **Mother God,**
which we on Earth have only tasted
aspects of…
In short,
**Oh, Friends of the ages,
demand the Healing
of our collective emotional body
to be able to experience
the Return of this Love.**

148°

Cohorts of Freedom,
within the Cooperative Endeavor
of Love's great Plan
oftentimes Humanity's attention
takes a less efficient pathway
unto her eventual goals for a next step.
**Remembering that,
EVERYONE makes it, eventually.**
Sufficient to the day-why you are here-is
to use the breath and the "still, small Voice":
"Light Expand,
Light Expand...
Light take hold,
Light Command..."
Because the Earth (and other planets close by)
is about to go through a severe initiation,
the amount of Light the cells (you and I)
emit is the *only* measure that Cosmic Law
(the big "cats") can use to gauge
their flow.... Understand?

All being One:
The amount of emotional healing-or not-that
has taken place will determine the amount of
"severity" that the return to LOVE will require.
Make no mistake. These are the Big Breaths and
This is the Miracle Moment. Now is The Time.

*Light Expand, Light Command,
Light I Am, Everywhere Present.*

I Am the being of Light.

149°
Wise Ambassadors

Great, Great Light, gentle readers,
as we endeavor to expand, embody, express,
and experience the greatest shift
any planet and race has ever witnessed,
it may serve to remember that
next to the separation (Purity) taking place,
the full "growing-up" of the sixth and seventh
root races – already here as young adults – and the
"on camera" re-connection with
the Elemental Beings and Angels
(not to mention the ET's of all varieties and *more*)
is a stage set for everything from flipped-out chaos
to jaw-dropping Peace and Comfort.

So, the main ingredient
that the Cosmic/Universal Law is hoping to use
is enough Love and Its Law of Harmony in action
among the Causal Leaders of the continents.

For instance, on camera: top office leaders,
using the Power of the spoken *Wisdom of Love,*
demonstrating the actions that move us towards
"a New Way on a New Earth for a New Humanity,"
encompassing a cabinet of new minded leaders
who refer to the core of Justice
as being plenty for all.

There is much to Visualize.

I Am an Ambassador of Love.

I Am the Light of the World
and I Bless this Planet now.

150°
Sex and the Moment at Hand

As most are aware: There are
Great Cosmic, Grand (new) Solar Rays
pouring into our Earth, et al.
Many of Them are programmed
with the Cosmic Heart of Mother God;
all that Cosmic Love is the activity of creation.
This is a "heads-up memo" regarding one way
the feeling of this return to Cosmic Love
may be experienced by some.
It most likely will be received or otherwise directed
towards (as thoughts and "reasons" for) sex.
It is understandable when you think it through.
The darker contingency
that wishes and needs presences/souls to survive
has invested much already into this forecast
and its inevitability.
Here is a quote from Universal I AM
regarding this foreseen situation.

"Be very aware that the subtle,
and not so subtle,
pushy reasons to have sex
will be prevalent everywhere now.
It is the ego (and its lower vibrational aspects that
still need to know the Truth and its healing Power)
that is running that show.
It won't find it there.
And with time "running-out,"
some will find themselves tricked into a world
that may take many cycles of embodiment
to free themselves of.
Be diligent in your guard…"

151°

Co-Servers, we love to be where Love is.
Through the open Heart
directed by that clear Mind
we move about our given day,
free and available
to the behest of the Divine Plan
and toward the expectation of Happiness.

An Invocation may be:

My Great God Self, oh Beloved all That I AM,
which I Am.
Come forth and fill, flood, and charge
our whole outer life
with every Quality of the Universal I AM,
which desires to live free on Earth.
I ask from my Heart
that my third eye,
my clear inner sight, be opened,
that I may see clearly the Truth
that surrounds me.

I choose Peace and I demand this outer self
be the Full embodiment and expression
of my wholly Ascended Self.
See to it that I Am working
daily and constantly
with the Angels and Elementals
for the New Earth
and our Children's safe and Perfect Freedom.

This is my Joy and my Blessing,
and I Am so very grateful!

152°

Star Walkers, the Cosmic Love
that is the reality now superseding all others
is the great Victory of the whole of Heaven,
to witness now unfolding through us, in daily life.
Just the term spoken, "Cosmic Love,"
has transfiguring power that triggers
and sets abuzz even legions of your ancestors
within the Starships around Earth.

Gentle readers,
there is a longstanding gift
from the heart of God
given through the Mighty Elohim
and, of course, any assisting Master
you wish to invite.
It is the action and substance of
"Cosmic Christ Illumining Love,"
or "Wisdom," or "Power," or "_____."

***I call upon that Cosmic Christ
Illumination to assist in this way.***

Any who will try this, in fundamental mastery,
will experience its great activity
directly in the Mind and Feelings.
It is a Gift with a guarantee!
It is Love that woke you up this morning.

***I Am the Presence
and Its intelligent activity,
blessing all that I contact.***

I am so grateful.

153°

Forcefields of Love Divine, to Light only do I bow.
You know, one of our Prime Directives
is to build and establish a renewed
Illumined Atmosphere of Spiritual Freedom
for the mass of Humanity to *choose* and flourish
within as a refuge during the changes
and as a choice of continuous development.

The easiest and Happiest way to accomplish this
moment-to-moment is through developing
a rhythmic flow of ***Adoration*** back to our
Universal, Individual, great God Self.
This aspect of you does not look upon your discord
or lack. It only realizes flow, the in- and out-breath.
It/You, on this level, simply projects
a Ray of Life-Force to you here.
There is much to learn.

What is so very ***important now***
is efficient FLOW and the short-cut to *That* is,
to give a projection of your heart's Pink Flame
back to your Cosmic Self;
who wishes to somehow be
the only acting presence here. Because…
It hears the Earth's Call for assistance, Now.

Oh beloved of my Soul, I Love You.
Flame within my Heart, Open, Expand, and
Project the Feeling of Loving Gratitude
back to my beautiful God Self constantly.
Bring this to my outer mind's attention often,
that I may amplify this activity
on behalf of all life's Freedom
here on Earth. I love You!

154°

Beloved Masters, as the world of daily life
continues to change completely,
it is the better part of Wisdom to remind each other
that the Perfection of Being is our destiny.
It begins with loving, knowing, and
remembering the River of Life
as a great stream of Electronic Life-force that
flows into my Being from the Central Suns.
It is also my own heart's Flame,
as my own Central Sun.
This River refracts as if passing through a prism
and my Solar Chakras take form,
each one, a Sun in its own Truth.
Each Chakra having a set of
reasons and plans for being.
The River then cascades into
each of my 12 major Meridians,
then pouring into each of my billions of Cells.
Each one a Temple,
with a center (Heart Sun),
a group of ministers (mitochondria),
and on and on this River Flows;
out, Out into every aspect of other life
that I contact just by my thought,
and love, to it.

I let go of the thought process
and I Feel and simply AM this River.

The River of Life flows in.
The Ocean of Life is within.
Divine Creation ensues...
and I Am a Divine Director
of this Sacred Fire and Holy Water.

155°

There is nothing more important
than your I Am-ness.

There is nothing more real than the Ascension.

There is no thing "bigger" going on
in the whole of creation,
than this moment on Earth.

Q) How are you?...

A) I Am outrageously blessed.

*Oh great God-Self
and Holy Spirit,
flood my entire being and world
with every activity
of Sacred Fire necessary
to keep my Heart open
through this great
Worldwide and Galactic upgrade.
May I be of the greatest assistance
to anybody and any thing I contact.*

156°

From the very Mind of Prime Creator,
you, beloved, have come forth as a replica of Its Self.
You can have anything you want,
when you ask it from the Heart.
Our Heart is God's Heart, the same.

Life is so beautiful.
Life is so unstoppable.
Life wants only to Bless you.

The Transformation of Humanity,
how we will be after the shifts,
is one in service,
giving back to the Universal
in many ways.

Of course as you know so well,
we have, long ago, begun this...

Decree:

I Am the Light of the World.
All of the World is within me.
All of the World is Light.

I thank you.

157°

Rivers of life, we bring to and for each other
that which is more than necessary,
the greatest gift to ourselves,
the gift of divine friendship
and its communion – together.
With this truth, today I wish to ponder
the flawless dispensation and perfection
of *what I put my Attention on also ascends.*
This Mercy to life comes as an "add on"
to the **Law of Life:**
*Where my attention goes my Energy flows
and there I show up or there I Am.*
This is worth our pointed contemplation
because it is part of Life's great Mercy
to all other life needing assistance.

For a moment, see and feel your Heart Flame,
Its Sacred Fire. Watch it rise up into your head.
Now see this create and balance
a beautiful oval sphere over your entire Being.
Our service is to direct – from here –
our attention anywhere,
to anyone who may need assistance
to assure their conscious Ascension.
All this just by seeing this activity
and placing my thought there.

***I Am here, I Am there,
and I Am the only presence acting.
I Am the only authority.***

When the above is used with any momentum,
you may know that a great company
of Angels and Elementals work with you.

158°

Precious of the Stars,
do you realize how wonderful this Plan is?
The plan of ***the full reunification of all life
on the surface of Earth.***

The blueprint for Earth is:
Humans, *bridging in daily collaboration*
with Angels* and Elemental Beings**
expand in unbridled creativity.
Now the next step is
to include the many Star nations,
the Galactics and other Celestials.
Be with this, when you can.

Feel the choice of your Mother/Father Earth
to have a gathering of the many,
hosted upon Her body.
Note your feelings of seeing some "others"
who look nothing like Humans.
Do you think the Human-looking ones will arrive
before the "chaotic shifting" or after,
when those of us who wished, *who chose to depart,*
have gone?

***I Am an Ambassador of Love.
I Am the Divine Plan In action.
No weapon prospers
against our younger generation.
"I AM" the Authority.***

* The breath of Source, the feeling Beings.

** There are several graded orders/levels
of the Elementals/Mental Power Beings.

159°
Spring-like Earth

Beloved of the Light,
there is one who desires to bring more
of her assistance to you and your bodies
and to all upon my surface:
She is the great Goddess of Eternal Spring:

"I Am privileged to be a part
of this Metamorphosis in the heavens
of this dear planet and system of Worlds in need.
Some of you know me
as the Goddess of Resurrection.
I was a part of the setting into order and flow
of the patterns of lifeforce on your dear Earth.
We wish for you all to know
that a great confluence and procession
of entirely new Ecology and environments
are rapidly interfacing with that which has been.
For instance, the melting of the polar ice caps,
which is part of the return of a surface experience
free of temperature extremes, is interfacing with
legitimate discord and its climate crisis.
I wish for you to *Feel* the deserts blooming
and the poles also.
There is much that we are–as a matter of
course–not allowed to chat about, quite yet.
Though please *Feel* your seat on this Council."

I Am the Solar Being
and I Am the Divine Plan,
breathing and smiling,
my reason for being here.

160°
A Voice of Earth

I breathe with you and sometimes for you.
With the need of the hour now being
one of *knowing* and having
a clear and rhythmic Vision
of what New Daily Life shall be,
your determined choice is
that *Harmony* be your True Power.
We go forward at exponential speed
into the expression of Crystalline bodies
of Indestructible Light Substance.
Visualize and Feel this actuality, beloveds.
Pretend!

The Goddess of Eternal Spring continues...
"For those who wish to know a part of the science
used to assure our Victorious out-picturing
of the new globally temperate and elementally
perfect playground we all wish for as Daily Life,
the Hawaiian Islands (for one)
have and hold certain areas
where a human has never intruded –
except by atmospheric discord –
or interfered with the beloved Elementals
and their order of creative expression and Joy.
We needed a pattern in place from which to expand....
This has been Victoriously guarded
and is underway Now, friends."

I Am the New Earth in her New Axis,
spinning in the New Heavens.
Freedom's love.

161°

Cohorts of Power,
in that enthusiasm
that lifts all we could possibly contact,
we breathe deeply together.
This "blockbuster show" of all shows in the Galaxies
that happens to be headquartered here on Earth
is nothing short of a great Cosmic Climax.
One of the reasons for
holding Harmony in the Feelings
(which means holding open the Heart – crucial
to our Now Moment)
is that the human structure
holds memories of closing
or shutting down the Heart
during *changes of Cosmic Cycles*.
Even the minor ones are littered
with memories of destruction.
We prove this in recording history
by the collapse of certain ages and so on.

It is a choice of Power to ask for assistance
to help you keep the Heart open
and to have your attention held
upon Perfect Memories.
The fearful memories are held in the
Etheric Body's records and wish to be Purified,
hence the consummate use of the Sacred Fire.

All of the Light Realms will assist you greatly
in this endeavor.

162°

I prompt myself to consider
The Remembering,
as a seasoned practitioner would
in the activity of assistance
to a new mother and her spouse,
during the travails of birthing.
To remember and see
only the successes of the process.

Also, I remember to move or act swiftly
from a poised and masterful place
of knowing and reminding the ones present
of the new life (embodiment) they are a part of.

And above all things it is
to maintain harmony in the feelings,
so that Love's Power can manifest instantly
anything for us.
It is that serene or not often shaken stance
of the Harmony of our Total True Being
that already is ours and Earth's certain victory.

163°

Lovers of Peace, as you breathe,
and sigh a "happy to be here sigh,"
in your bright visions today, we as a group
could be of rich service to the Great Plan
by connecting with the children
and the entire younger generation.
They not only will be going through
the experience of watching complete systems
collapse and dissolve, but will have
the responsibility of staying in Harmony.
They have much to be busy about,
"our young ones," on every continent.
Part of our great service to their mission is
to *Cause* the Angels and other God Forces
to protect and be immediately close
to those Re-Builders.

Also, remember
You are a vast multidimensional
God Being of great Light
and by your realizing that, you know,
you can have anything *You* want.
Remember also, it is the God Power in you,
as you – the director. Yes?
Better to be God now, than later. Yes!
...I Am That, I AM!

I Am the One thinking these thoughts.
I Am Feeling the Great Ones nurture
and protect our youth, everywhere!

164°

Invocation:

Oh majestic Infinite Light! Ever unfolding Song!
Fill, flood, and charge into and through
every activity I interface with this day,
known or unknown.
Come forth in ever expanding waves,
reach out beyond my perceived aura
and lift every other activity of life
that I continually contact.
My dearest demand is that my entire outer self
be an ever-increasing reservoir and fountain
of Cosmic Love Supreme.
So it is, that I call upon
the great Goddess of Venus Herself
to enfold and expand the Sacred Fire
of *Her* Cosmic Love Supreme
as a miracle mantel upon me,
to assist all that my atmosphere touches
Moment to moment, and Cause This
to be expanded and sustained.

*I Am the great creative Heart of God.
What I visualize...Is Real.*

Remember:
A reason for meditation is
to Feel the Love of Source.

165°
Gaia's Message

Bless you,
I Am the Voice of your beloved planet Gaia.

I wish to speak to you
who are and have been like my children,
some of you for so very long.
I have not spoken much over the Ages,
but now is now.
If I may be of assistance, I will be brief.

For those of you that are in female embodiment,
please consider getting some Sun
upon your breasts this season – those in the
Northern Hemisphere or those down South,
do not delay.

Men, please practice some Adoration
to my Elements in any way.

Men and Women get out into my gifts to you
and live Love: Bless and Admire.
Please, go out into Nature
in any way that you can think of.
Be imaginative.

Use your Free Will
and experience something in this:
*your final embodiment upon my body's bulk
in this dimensional existence,*
for the Vehicle called Earth,
as you know/knew it,
is in reality no more.

I have moved onward.
Mercy and Its Great Cosmic Host
have allowed me a sufficient lag time
until the form you call physical
out-pictures the Cause.
Be prepared to be happy –
you who have not yet experienced our trees,
night sky, creeks, and meadows, beloveds.

My Love carries you forward. Together.

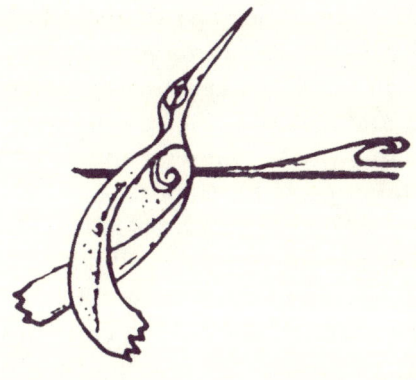

I pour forth all of my

Love
    Gratitude
        and Blessing

To all of Nature

For sustaining me

Here on Earth

Throughout the centuries.

166°

Gentle Masters, our brave ones,
this is a reminder to breathe,
utilizing the conscious breaths
that serve you the best.
Then try some other sorts as well.
Adding tone or movement will greatly assist you
to be an I AM Presence in residence.
As we all move closer to the shifting of Earth's axis,
it is our service to shift our axis first
into the New Axis of New Humanity.
This is the service of the hour, beloveds.
*To consciously–through your Energy
and Vibration*–play with the idea
and feeling of being a pioneer,
to clear the way for yourself and those (all life)
who cannot do so for themselves at this time.
You need this, beloveds.
This is one of the tangible "all hands on deck"
sounds moving through Ascending Humanity.
The sound of **service to the whole,**
through playing or pretending the New, Now.

Just breathe, move, and act with thought,
your spine full of light,
your inner Sun ruling all cellular structure,
your Lifestream (river of Light)
that enters your crown pouring directly
through you into the Earth's center.
And on and on you go,
with a great Host of Angelic Beings
walking, breathing, and smiling with you.
In service.

167°

Since mid-August, 2000, it was Decreed and set:
that all children coming in would be
of the Crystalline, "Manifester" variety.
Though we would find it hard to swallow
upon seeing their resume in works accomplished
in other star systems.

The time for Earth to move into diamond quality
Light Substance is coming down "the canal."
"Now" is the only word for when this will transpire
and.... Now.

Can you feel the great accomplishments
we have anchored into place for this New Being?
Specifically, the mighty Magnet
of the Pink Sacred Fire?

You see, all the other activities of the Sacred Fire,
the Blue Lightning shattering of old structures,
the Violet of balanced Purity,
the Green of Illumined Truth
and Concentration...
have been set and are flourishing.
All of these are mostly "Causal" in this Divine Plan,
though when the Pink Flame and Ray,
which is the Magnet and Effectual,
establishes itself here...
well, now the fun begins.

168°
You, The Christ

"See only the Christ in each other"
and
"Add not a feather's weight
to humanity's burden at this time."

As of Now, these are as important
to our own individual Freedom in the Ascension
and the Divine Plan as the breath itself.

It is not easy to refrain from forming opinions
of others and of things that are happening.

This is a "fine tune" request
from the great Cosmic In-breath
and from the Office of the Christ.
"The Christ" is the word that means
a consciousness that hath no impure thing in it.
Saint Germain has said,
"Get off the opinion highway
and onto the Ascension highway."

We strive for the greatest Illumination
of all Humanity at this moment.
We choose to see, feel, and know the New Earth.
What fun, beloveds.
During any culmination of ages
into next expression,
everything is heightened and amplified.

Return time within the Law of the Circle
is tightened and shortened.

169°
The Away Team

As some of you are aware,
the muti-galactic Ascension into new expression
has already happened,
even as Earth's population is awaited.
Much like a great wedding event
where everybody is at the chapel,
the reception caterers have the food hot
and the bar chilled,
though the bride is not quite prettied up yet.
Everybody is waiting...
some patient, some not so patient.

The perfect re-written script is
that a number of us would embody,
by actualizing our seven chakras' truth,
the Christed Planetary Being.
By devotion to that,
we naturally embody the next step:
Solar Being, which is the return
to our "First Expression,"
only now, with all the Illumination
of the successful experiment
of planetary Mastery –
Love's perfect presence
in cohort with Angels and Elementals.

This is called the Great Cosmic In-breath.
The "Away Team" ensures Its success.

170°
Being in Your Dignity

Unto us, whom only Love could pull, I sing.
As the phenomenal convergence
of all the rivers and tributaries of everything
that must play out here on Earth continues...
You are advised to get close and stay near
to the still-point that you truly are.
Let me elaborate on this.

Life as it is, is "phenomenal."
When I have a relationship with the unfathomable,
and a moment to stand in awe of That,
which is Life's majesty happening,
then, I know that I know,
that what is unjust is folly.

You see, beloveds, the fiats,
"Where my Attention is, there I Am"
and, "What I meditate on I become"
have been given a great Dispensation
for the rest of Humanity
who may not be doing this for themselves
at this moment – the Great Cosmic In-breath.
Think for a moment how
"the few are doing for the many."

I Am empty of self.
I Am one with the Way.
The Way is all-inclusive.

171°
The Perfection of Being

As we (all) stand now,
Ascended and Free on Our New Earth
KNOWING the Truth:
that we "work" from/within
the realm of Cause alone.
We work and Stand in Consciousness –
dictating Reality...

Our Heart "goes radical" with the Archangels.
Our Mind soars with the Elohim and Elementals.
Our 12-fold Solar Chakras and full Solar Reality
as an ever changing matrix
of Great moving liquid Light Substance
carries this planet and the human race
rapidly forward in profound Solar Speed.

Unconditional Love,
Universal Wisdom,
and
Spiritual Power

Manifesting the Perfection of Being
across all aspects and dimensions of human activity,
from cooking to international finance,
from gardening to enormous World affairs.

Thank God for God.
I Am the only Presence acting!

172°

Flawless Dancers of the Sacred Fire,
in continuity with our conversation on
Harmonizer Cells and their/our activity:
As some may know,
We, in the planetary facet of the Plan,
have successfully created a Forcefield of Divine Love
(and its distinct children or different aspects).
Within this is the great Forcefield
of Elemental Protection,
while Metamorphosis is underway,
as in a cocoon,
or as an embryo to a human being.

Here's the unprecedented part:
Time and space are collapsing.
All seasons (summer, autumn, winter, and **Spring**)
are playing out for the whole population.
The great overlighting Devas wish to protect
and assure that that which is the New Picture
or New Show remain in vibrant health,
while pulling back or constricting flow
to that which is *willfully* in conflict
with the New Show.
This is why not adding a feather's weight
to others burdens, in any subtle way,
is vital to your complete and total Freedom.
High Science.

I Am the Harmony of my Total True Being.
I Am the being of Light and Love alone.

173°

Dearest Friends, in That Love
that knows no opposite and the Joy
of being a partner in cooperative service
with other groups from other systems, I share.

Some of the great Leaders of Rays (Chohans, etc.)
have called themselves "Angel Devas."
For instance, Saint Germain and Jesus are
Angel Deva of the Violet Fire
and Angel Deva of the Cosmic Christ.

Well, then there is the Angel Deva
of the Mother God.
This one is the Out-breath,
Feeling Consciousness to evolving life.
The very Presence of Mother God Herself.
The reason I bring this up is that
some of you/us have a "program"
to bring this to Nature, or to Humanity,
or any other part of life that you may pass by.

One could simply say:
***I call upon the Angel Deva
of the Mother God's Love to Nature
to pour through me today
and be the Full Presence of her Love
to Heal, Resurrect, and set free,
every Being of the Elements
that my Aura contacts,
and my Heart's Love, forever.***

174°

Embodied Co-Servers, perhaps a moment together in the Halls of Remembrance, with regards to the Simplicity of accomplishing the complex science (act) of the *Metamorphosis and Transfiguration of the Species*.

° All life ascends into or unto its next step. Regardless, so to speak.

° The term "bio-photonic energies" refers accurately to this jaw-dropping act of a God (Good)-Force overtaking and superseding unto next expression, which BTW, is sometimes an act of wiping off and etherealizing its Self/self. So, "bio-photonic" is an activity of Higher or Solar expressions as new cells are literally showing up on the spot, like an ambulatory group of medics in a conflict zone, performing heroic feats for *the surroundings-others*. We call them "Harmonizer Cells."

° The *act* of *drinking more water* than usual and blessing *with your feelings* that Universal Substance is your part in this medical activity.

° The unimaginable Intelligence of the Light Now entering Earth is stepped down and offered to you by the Plant Life (not "white meat" or "fish") to ingest and assimilate. (Check this through your Self.)

° Standing up and a quick raising of the arms and *breathing differently* help tremendously. It is the swift spontaneous doing of something different, like *breathing, that re-programs self* **for something big.**

175°

Beams of Hope, you who are the particles
of the Fragrance of Stellar Fountains,
I Am the Voice of the Elohim.
For those here who wish it,
there is a Vision of something
that is of high wattage power
and readily available for the aspirant.
It is the full spectrum of the Opalescent Fire
and its Ray of Transformation,
Transfiguration, and Rejuvenation.
Be it said that the Transformation most required
for Humanity at large is one back to Loving service
to all Life, nature, the lower evolutions,
and other races of your "kind."
Though many of you are there already!
What this Transfiguring Ray also has
is unlimited intelligence
for the atomic/cellular Rejuvenation
of your physical garments.
The shortcut for this blessing is:
Look in your mirror and declare your I Am–present.
Sing Your I Am That,
Perfect health and eternal youth.
Smile, and *ask* for all the assistance available
to make you a fountain and reservoir of the Opal Fire.
Then visualize this Gift any way you wish
from within you and out from you to be sustained.
Your smiling Harmony will testify to your truth.

176°
It Would Seem

Mighty Rods and Circles of Power,
Harmony that you truly are,
allow for a brief concept
with regards to our cohesive Mission
of Healing Humanity and Earth's systems.

We would acknowledge that
back in the year 2000, and then again in 2004,
the United States of the Americas elected
(or did not *refuse*)
the placement and re-placement
of a rather conflict-oriented regime,
into the governing Executive Branch.
We mention this now,
that you might more deeply *Understand*
the reasons why "things" have not progressed,
as we certainly had Hoped.

You may know that the ***Initiations***
we each and all–family, region, nation,
hemisphere, Global–are passing (or not)
are just that; *Initiations* "back" ***to Love.***
The point being:
It would seem that a nation failed one initiation.
Because at some point, a nation (family, region)
must *Stand Shoulder to Shoulder*
as the ***Light of Love's controlling Presence,***
as the *action of Justice,*
as a pattern for the rest of Humanity.

If this be not so, then I have missed
understanding something here.
Because a needed portion of the population
has not, as of yet, stood forth
and demonstrated what is
Universal Law-Love's governorship,
a set of contingency plans that have been
activated and put into motion.

The Great Ones, the Devas, continue to step in,
to cleanse and purify us, the atmosphere,
and all the elements.
Our collective emotional body's healing is the gauge
the Great Ones use moment-to-moment
as the determining factor
for how much the oceans may slosh.

Our directive, what we must do is
hold the Harmony and Blaze the Light.
As in: ***I Am the Harmony of my Total True Being-being. For all.***
The former is mentioned so that we may have
a thankful reminder of what matters, Now.

177°
Cosmic Beauty

From the Land of Peace we have created
in thought and feeling,
the Land of Love's Joy,
Spiritual Freedom in progress.
Let us be in actual presence.

Like the Archangels, we are created
in the full splendor of Mother/Father God.
We are angelic,
in every way able to breathe with
and assist every other facet and aspect
of the Jewel of creation.
Like the Elohim, we are fully endowed
with tangible Cosmic Call,
known to you as Divine Mind
or Cosmic Consciousness.
Connected.

Literal Children/extensions
of the Large Suns of the Galaxy, you are.
The Cosmic Truth of your Being has
within it the Divine Plan for Humanity's
inclusion in the great Ascension.
It is a program to *"forget"*
the long destructive activity
and the baggage of returning to...
and returning to...
all the blah blahs about it.
"It" has become, *literally,*
a transmuted floral arrangement
and feeling of propulsion
into wild happiness
that we are ***in, Now.***

*I am a Crystal Mountain Range,
still watering, fertilizing,
and protecting
the living-rooms and bedrooms
of the valley "below."*

*Everything the Archangels are,
That I AM.
Everything the Elohim are,
That I AM.
Everything the Ascended Masters are,
That I AM.
I Am the Giver, giving.
And I Am the entire
New Age of Freedom.
Cheers.*

178°
Two Mothers

Interstellar Masters of Grace,
You, who are the answers:
I thank you for the Purity
and your ***devotion*** to the much
that has been asked of you
in this enormous mission.
Some of you are aware that Mother Mary
has assumed the identity of my *Siamese Twin*.
We are joined at the shoulder, so to speak.
So it is that we answer the same calls
and are one in that respect.
Also it must come to some of you
that the Great Planet/Star of Venus
has long been thoroughly committed
to a tangible and direct bodily influence with me
until my/our full Freedom in the Ascension.

Now, within these two activities is to come
both of their individual next revelations.
For you must come to the experience of
Consciousness dictates Reality.

So, the mountains around my surface
will be the starters of these "revealings"
unto the world of surface life.
Please keep visualizing
Freedom in daily life – on Main Street.

Your love is wonderful.
I Am a voice of Gaia.

179°
The Voice of Many

Great Friends, Co-Servers, interstellar relations,
as it has been my privilege to carry this Light
and experience its expansion in service to the All,
I/We do bow deeply before the great Ray of Devotion
and Constancy in each of you who have carried
and enflamed their sphere of influence.

I Am grateful, I Am grateful, I Am so very grateful.

We ask that this affirming and declaring
be one of your staples in Feeling
as we hold steady in the Harmony
that is our Magnet for all others
still seeking the Light.

I am the one Voice of *Many* and I affirm with You:

*I Am the full manifestation of Grace,
the action of Divine Love,
transforming Humanity at this time.*

*I Am the Mother/Father God,
having reclaimed this sweet Earth,
and I Am the only authority.*

180°

B,B,B,B

Well, beloveds,
being that we are together,
and that we have made our choice
to Stand in The Light,
I wish to finalize, with *You,*
a few thought forms
that we have authored together
in our new Book of Life,
for your planet and your Children.
I speak both as one with you in the body
and as one from the Light Realms.

Like the prodigal child,
long has been your *journey* "out there."
In reality, perhaps, *that* is over for you.
You are Free. Always.
Being Now.
You have come back Home
to Love and Its Light…

~ We are, and will be, the life-preserver
to those whom we are here to serve.

~ The seas of daily life
on the surface will get a bit rough,
perhaps even exceedingly rough,
for a spell, for the many.

~ Eternally, *we* are the *Stillness:*
active for the many.

~ Like the Lotus, we are
the *double picture of **Service to the Many.***
That being so, we are connected
to the mud and murky bottom
of human creation (our long root).
The underwater part of our connection
is a picture of the quiet beneath the surface
of the waves of the outer. Understand?

~ We are the *Thousand-Petaled Blossom
of perfect manifestation* on the same surface.
Only that our thoughts and feelings are elsewhere!

~ *"I Am the total embodiment of Love"*
is the Affirmation for *the Illumination*
of our street-wise humanity,
those who have chosen Peace and plenty
for all, on "Main Street."

About the Author

Yoj has devoted his life to receiving

"the greatest Light (*intelligence*)
of the greatest Love (*cohesive power* of All)
for the greatest good and the highest Vision
for Earth and all Humanity."

Though he knew and felt that what he had asked for had already been given to Humanity, he persevered on his journey of discovery and became a Messenger for the Light in his own unique style.

He declared his wish to be a pure and clear channel and during a moment with one of the great Goddesses was told: "Regarding your true desire, we wish you to know this is who and what you are already. So beloved, let this be your decree:

***I Am a server of Humanity
and I Am the being of Light.***"

Yoj states, "I have returned to this one statement rhythmically."

Yoj lives in Mount Shasta, California. He is an avid river kayaker, forest and mountain hiker, ecstatic dancer, and free-heel, full mountain skier.

He is physically active in a work-a-day life running a garden maintenance business during the warmer seasons and working outdoors all winter as "The Eco Man," doing the hands-on recycling at Mount Shasta Ski Park. All redemption monies from his efforts are donated to a few worthy environmental projects by the Ski Park owners.

As an alternative to automobiles, Yoj is a distributor of electrically assisted bicycles. He enjoys visiting and offering assistance to local elders. For Yoj, it's about the joy.

And last, but not least, Yoj is a long-time devotee to one or two cookies a day.

To read more of Yoj's messages, go to:
www.streetwiseascension.info

Email: streetwise@snowcrest.net

Mount Shasta Light Publishing Publications

These publications can be purchased:

- Directly from us by phone
  or at our mailing address
- From our secure shopping cart on our website:
  http://www.mslpublishing.com
- From Amazon.com
- Bookstores through New Leaf Book Distributing

If ordering by mail, contact us for shipping charges.

Mount Shasta Light Publishing
P.O. Box 1509
Mount Shasta, CA 96067-1509
USA

aurelia@mslpublishing.com

Phone: 530-926-4599

(If no answer, please leave a message)

Mount Shasta Light Publishing Publications

Street·Wise Ascension $13.00

The Seven Sacred Flames $39.00

Seven Sacred Flames Prayer Booklet $7.00

Ascension Activation Booklet $7.00

Seven Sacred Flames Card Deck $16.00

Telos Book Series Card Deck $16.00

Telos – Volume 1
Revelations of the New Lemuria $18.00

Telos – Volume 2
Messages for the Enlightenment
of a Humanity in Transformation $18.00

Telos – Volume 3
Protocols of the Fifth Dimension $20.00

The Effects of Recreational Drugs
on Spiritual Development $4.00

Angelo's Message – Angelo, the Angel Cat
Speaks to all People on this Planet
Regarding the Treatment of Animals $8.00

Las Siete Llamas Sagradas $24.00

El folleto de siete llamas sagradas $7.00

El folleto de la ascensión de la llama $7.00

Telos – Libro 1
Revelaciones de la Nueva Lemuria $18.00

Telos – Libro 2
Mensajes para la iluminación de una
humanidad en transformación $18.00

Telos – Libro 3
Protocolos de la quinta dimensión $20.00

Song of Things to Come

As the ancient Hopi trail song says,
"...the trail ends in Beauty."